THE AMERICAN
COLLEGE
PRESIDENCY
AS VOCATION

THE AMERICAN
COLLEGE
PRESIDENCY
AS VOCATION

Easing the Burden, Enhancing the Joy

WILLIAM V. FRAME

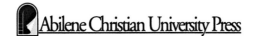Abilene Christian University Press

THE AMERICAN COLLEGE PRESIDENCY AS VOCATION
Easing the Burden, Enhancing the Joy

Copyright 2013 by the Council of Independent Colleges

ISBN 978-0-89112-385-9
LCCN 2012036752

Printed in the United States of America

Scripture quotations, unless otherwise noted, are from The Holy Bible, New International Version. Copyright 1984, International Bible Society. Used by permission of Zondervan Publishers. Scripture quotations noted RSV are taken from the Revised Standard Version of the Bible, copyright 1952 [2nd edition, 1971] by the Division of Christian Education of the National Council of the Churches of Christ in the United States of America. Used by permission. All rights reserved.

Published in association with the Council of Independent Colleges, Washington, DC.

LIBRARY OF CONGRESS CATALOGING-IN-PUBLICATION DATA
Frame, William V.
The American college presidency as vocation : easing the burden, enhancing the joy / William V. Frame.
     pages cm
ISBN 978-0-89112-385-9
1. Universities and colleges--United States--Administration. 2. College presidents--United States. 3. Educational leadership--United States. I. Title.
LB2341.F68 2013
378.1'11--dc23
                              2012036752

Cover design by Rick Gibson
Interior text design by Sandy Armstrong

For information contact:
Abilene Christian University Press
1626 Campus Court
Abilene, Texas 79601

1-877-816-4455 toll free
www.abilenechristianuniversitypress.com

Table of Contents

Introduction

The Project

One splendid July afternoon in 2008, on the patio in front of The Lodge at Glendorn near Bradford, Pennsylvania, ten of us had just adjourned the initial meeting of the final seminar of the Presidential Vocation and Institutional Mission Program and we wondered how to memorialize the achievements of the program. Joel Cunningham, then vice chancellor of the University of the South, and his wife, Trudy, were there. So were Mary Ann Dillon, president of Mount Aloysius College; Richard Hughes, then leading the Boyer Center at Messiah College; Richard Ekman, president of the Council of Independent Colleges (CIC) and his senior colleagues Hal Hartley and Barbara Hetrick; and Anne Frame and I. All but Barbara had been involved with the program from its beginnings in the summer of 2005.

Richard Hughes won the toss with the suggestion of a publishable manuscript modeled on *Habits of the Heart* and *The Good Society* by Robert Bellah and others. Bellah and his co-authors had used extensive conversations with thoughtful Americans from a range of professions and regions to illustrate practical strategies for how to live rightly and well in the presence of both the virtues and the "destructive consequences" of "American individualism." Since many of the participants in the program had told us that vocational considerations had helped them in just these ways with their lives and work in America's colleges and universities, Richard's suggestion seemed especially apt.

In the months that followed, Richard and I prepared a proposal to CIC for a 150–200 page publication that I would write and Richard would edit. It was to rely upon ninety-minute interviews with one-third of the 210 individuals who had participated in the Presidential Vocation and Institutional Mission seminars to record the impact of the program upon the practice of the American college and university presidency. It would also illustrate the discoveries we had made in the course of the inquiry about vocation itself, the process of discernment, and the advantages and risks of "alignment" between the president's vocation and the institution's mission. The Lilly Endowment agreed in the fall of 2009 to fund the project, and the interviews of thirty-five couples and individuals selected from among the program participants commenced in January 2010 at the CIC Presidents Institute on Marco Island, Florida.

The Program

The Presidential Vocation and Institutional Mission Program had grown from a report of the uses I had made of vocation at Augsburg College that appeared in the Review section of the *Chronicle of Higher Education* in September 2002. Written in the midst of the excitement stirred up among America's private colleges and universities by the Lilly Endowment's Program for the Theological Exploration of Vocation (PTEV), the article caught the attention of Rich Ekman and Rusty Garth, the executive vice president (now deceased) ofw CIC. Entitled "A President Looks Back 500 Years and Finds His Calling," my article reflected upon the applicability of vocation to college and university presidents—perhaps the only constituent class in the academy not specifically included in the discernment and exploration projects generated by the eighty-eight colleges and universities receiving PTEV grants from the Lilly Endowment.

As president of the national association for small and mid-sized independent colleges and universities, Rich Ekman invited me to a meeting with Craig Dykstra and Chris Coble at the Lilly Endowment in Indianapolis in the spring of 2004. The agenda was to explore the organization's interest in a program for college presidents, both those currently in office and those who might become prospective presidents, which would identify and develop the advantages for both colleges and presidents of better "alignment" between personal vocation and institutional mission.

At the meeting, Rich observed that the average tenure of sitting presidents in America's independent colleges and universities was falling toward the five-year average typical among public institutions. We both attested to the fact that more and more presidencies seemed to be ending badly as well as earlier. Complaints of exhaustion among college presidents seemed to each of us to be escalating, and we agreed that the changing demands of the work, even when accomplished, were not particularly fulfilling to presidents or uniformly restorative of institutional vitality. The college presidency seemed to be losing its traditional intellectual and civic leadership role and was being increasingly confined to development functions, the administration of operations, regulatory compliance, and trustee relations.

Drawing from my tiring but increasingly satisfying experience at Augsburg and from Rich's observations of particularly vibrant presidencies among CIC member institutions, we argued that sophisticated consideration of vocation by presidents in a retreat context with colleagues and spouses might very well reinvigorate them, extend their tenures, and restore the reach and fulfillment of their leadership. We thought the likelihood of these results would be enhanced by systematic attention to the alignment of the presidents' interests, talents, and principles with the traditions and purposes of the institutions they served. This, we believed, would impart a stronger sense of belonging to participating presidents that would, in turn, inspire more joyful leadership.

We argued that CIC was the right executor of this enterprise because the self-knowledge required for vocational discernment, along with the practical knowledge required of useful vocational service to campus and community, were profoundly compatible with the leadership support that distinguished CIC's highly acclaimed assistance to its burgeoning membership. Therefore we asked whether the Lilly Endowment would welcome a proposal from CIC to address shortening tenures and declining interest in becoming a president. We told Lilly that we envisioned a participative inquiry on personal vocation, institutional mission, and the alignment of the two for sitting presidents of CIC's membership and those whom these presidents hoped would one day join their ranks.

The Lilly Endowment encouraged CIC to submit an application to launch a vocation and mission program for presidents and prospective presidents in the summer of 2005. CIC's Fred Ohles, now president of Nebraska Wesleyan University, wrote the grant application for CIC and the Lilly Endowment approved it in the fall of 2004. We convened the first seminar—this one for presidents—at Airlie House, in Virginia in June 2005. A month later, we convened a second seminar at the same location—this one for aspiring presidents. In the meantime, we recruited twenty presidents and spouses, twenty prospective presidents and spouses, and seven facilitators in two teams; we assembled a curriculum (two packets of readings and two syllabi) and developed the meeting venue and scheduling details for each subsequent seminar.

The Program Curriculum

The most formative deliberation during this period for the program's design occurred at the Centers of Distinction, Wabash College, Crawfordsville, Indiana, in the Spring of 2005. Shirley Showalter, president emerita of Goshen College; Rich Ekman; Fred Ohles; Melanie Morey, senior director, NarrowGate Consulting; Douglas "Jake" Jacobsen, Distinguished Professor of Church History and Theology at Messiah College; and I spent two days (with the helpful counsel of others from Wabash and CIC) designing a curriculum that could be delivered in the seven plenary and four small-group sessions that made up the inaugural meeting of each seminar. We also sampled a wide range of readings. We emerged from that two-day deliberation with a four-subject curriculum—Vocation, Friendship, Institutional Mission, and Alignment of Personal Vocation with Institutional Mission. These subjects have guided the program from the beginning.

The premise of the curriculum is that work for which one is especially suited will be well and happily done. In the language of vocation, we said that being "called" to one's work yielded greater personal fulfillment and higher service to one's community than "choosing" one's work. From the beginning, therefore, we were convinced of a generic difference between vocation and career. But we knew that, even among us friends of vocation, there was little if any agreement concerning the origin and medium of the vocational call. Indeed, we knew that each of us had to remain open on these matters. Otherwise, we would be answering the fundamental question of the program ourselves instead of asking it of participants: "What is your vocation, and how do you know that you are accurately understanding and accommodating it?"

Hence, we asked potential participants in the program to provide a "personal statement" about their own vocational discernment. We looked to these statements for indications that their authors were curious about their own vocations as well as open to the distinction, albeit broad and unspecified, between career and calling. And we opened every seminar by asking each participant to introduce her or himself by explaining why one of the twenty short readings distributed ahead of the meeting had seemed particularly useful for the purposes of discernment. We then inquired about the subject of friendship on the assumption that discernment is unavoidably a social process. Whatever the origin of the "call," it is "received" in a "noisy" context and needs to be interpreted and translated with the help of caring and knowing friends—among whom spouses are often pivotal. (From the beginning, we used some of the letters of John and Abigail Adams to illustrate a bi-vocational and spousal relationship, which was of great value regarding discernment.)

We then turned to mission as the institutional equivalent of vocation for individuals and opened this segment of the inquiry with the help of Burton Clark's discussion of "saga" in his book, *The Distinctive College* (1970 and 1990). We explored this equivalency by laying a couple of Abraham Lincoln's speeches beside Alexis de Tocqueville's diagnosis of *Democracy in America* to confirm that both vocation and liberal education are counter-cultural in our democratic age. This exploration prepared us to wonder what relationship between the vocational president and the missional institution would be mutually sustainable.

Rusty Garth taught us to use "alignment" to describe this relationship, knowing that it should not be a "fusion" or "identity," on the one hand, nor a limited-term contract employing a president to administer a collegiate operation guided by an alien tradition, on the other.

All along the way, both in planning and facilitating the program, we held tightly to the conviction that vocational thinking and concepts were applicable to and useful for improving strictly secular lives and colleges. That conviction obliged us to embrace and protect a crucial ambiguity, namely, that the moral and ethical richness of vocation as a way of life for individuals and of mission as a way of life for colleges and universities had been born in theology but were surviving—indeed, prospering—in a democratic and secular age. Clearing away this ambiguity, either by ignoring the theological roots of vocation and mission or by denying their applicability to secular individuals and institutions, would have been irresponsible. At the earliest sign that participants were struggling with that ambiguity, we placed the issue high on the agenda of the one-on-one conversations with facilitators that were part of the seminars.

The Interviews

Before we began the conversations on which this book is based, I promised the program participants whom I interviewed that I would bring what I learned from them into view without violating their anonymity as individuals or exposing the identity of their employers. I have kept that promise, sometimes by creating composite characters of the presidents, prospective presidents, spouses, and institutions that I encountered; sometimes by changing the terms of particularly telling but singular stories; and by reaching for general categories—boards, faculties, and cabinets—whenever I could. With permission of the interviewees, I recorded and later transcribed my conversations with them. I used material from every interview somewhere in the book, sometimes to illustrate what seemed to me either non- (or even anti-) vocational thinking or action.

Although each of the six seminar programs was immediately acclaimed by a substantial number of its participants—often tearfully— as "among the best" they'd ever attended, the evidence as to whether the teachings of the program had taken up permanent residency in their lives and in the culture of their colleges and universities emerged only in the thirty-five conversations convened for the sake of this book.

In the course of these exchanges, stories turned up that were far more revealing than the short testimonials delivered in the course of the program—stories of personal vocation, institutional mission, and the alignment (or misalignment) of the two. And I seized hungrily on each one of these, sometimes adding my own testimonial or story, always pressing for deeper thought about the matter by asking questions such as, "What did that incident tell you—about yourself; the nature of academe; the burden of vocation; the critical importance (and rarity) of friendship?"

Thus, the interviews wandered down a trail marked by the six broad and interrelated questions—listed in Appendix IV—and sent to the interviewees in advance of each exchange. I stopped the conversations time and again to explore byways that promised deeper ground: "Doesn't that illustrate the distinction we've noticed between constituents and citizens; between service to profession and community; between calling and career?" Or: "How did you know that you had accurately discerned your vocation in that particular case and were pursuing it faithfully? How did you know that you accurately understood and were executing your institution's mission?" Or, yet again: "How have you aligned your vocation with the mission of your institution? Or have you merged them? What has this alignment or merger cost? How has it benefited you and your institution?"

During the ninety-minute sessions, these subjects came to life for both of us, just as they did in the seminars themselves. I can hear the rising interest and the occasional thrill of discovery in almost all of the voices preserved in my recordings of the interviews. And, I can see in the transcriptions of those recordings indications that all of us had acquired a lexicon that was tested and refined during the seminar conversations that allowed us to talk of life, work, and the American academy in unusually direct and profound ways.

Hence, no two conversations followed similar courses, covered the same questions, or absorbed the same amount of time. Yet, they were all the more valuable on account of these variations. In effect, they were custom fitted to the particular relationship that had developed between us in the program and in incidental meetings or conversations that grew from our participation in those seminars. Each interview got down to business very quickly, therefore, and each of us seemed to be looking for new frontiers in the issues we chose to explore.

Interviews conducted on the campus of a president or a dean were indistinguishable in tone or level of insight from those conducted at conferences or at some mutually convenient site. However, the ones on campuses to which I traveled remain memorable because of the setting. On a couple of occasions, my arrival coincided with a major campus event or a turning point in the life of the president or dean. These coincidences invariably crystallized or illustrated a particular aspect of vocation, and so each found its way into the manuscript at several points.

Only a couple of the conversations were of no more than passing interest to those whom I interviewed. In one instance, the interviewee complained that too many of the seminar enrollees were followers of Christianity. This, I was told, had led us away from the "professional discussion of the policies and actions of the presidency" and into irresolvable confusion about the "motives," "purposes," or "intentions" of such policies and actions. In the course of the program, we sometimes received the opposite complaint, namely, that secularists and agnostics would prevent us from situating the discussion "properly" on its Christian, even evangelical Protestant, foundations. Almost always, those who voiced either concern remembered it later as a misapprehension. The truth is that some of the most valuable contributions to the inquiry were made by agnostics, atheists, and also evangelical Christians.

All of the interviewees praised the program for extending the ambit of their friendships and collegiality, both of which were universally acknowledged by participants as necessary conditions of vocational discernment. Each requires a generosity of spirit and openness of mind that encourages the exploration of unfamiliar ideas, including their applicability to life and occupation.

The insights concerning vocation and related subjects explored in this book were drawn from the interviews, the seminar conversations, and the one-on-one exchanges I had with the members of the six "permanent groups" that Anne Frame and I facilitated. They are also drawn from my own presidency (at Augsburg College, 1997–2006) and from the many conversations I have had with friends and colleagues about vocation since I first met the idea in its classic form about twenty years ago.

To all those who participated in the seminars and the interviews, to the Council of Independent Colleges, to Lilly Endowment Inc., to the fifteen facilitators who joined me in pursuing the inquiry of the program, and to friends and counselors with whom I share an expanding wonderment at the transformative capacities of vocation, I issue a resounding, "Thank you!" To Richard Hughes, co-facilitator, theologian, profound partisan of vocation, and editor par excellence, I acknowledge a debt larger than I can repay. To Anne Lewis Frame I owe yet more, for her gracious audits of my thinking, for her remarkable understanding of the weight a presidency imposes on domestic life, and for our shared and loving search for right living.

William V. Frame
Tacoma, Washington
June 2011

CHAPTER 1

From Career to Calling
The Making of the Vocational President

More than twenty percent of the "prospective presidents" who enrolled in the Vocation and Institutional Mission Program were selected for a presidency either during or shortly after participating in the program. Every one of these "graduates" took the classic academic route to the presidency—from the professoriate through ascending administrative responsibilities, usually in the same institution, to candidacy for presidencies in church-related, regional, or another type of institution. Meeting them at the midpoint of this journey gave us in the program a rare glimpse into the processes by which teaching careers are typically converted from the classroom to academic administration. Interviewing this group one to three years later added insight, wherever it occurred, of the conversion from the professoriate to the vocational presidency. Being given a counseling role in these conversions as they actually were occurring was a great privilege: it provided a unique opportunity to witness the transitions that typically occur in this context and thus to identify the significant differences among career, profession, and vocation.

The program confronted these sojourners with the idea of vocation at an impressionable moment in their journeys—after their potential as vocationally oriented presidents had been flagged by presidents under whom they served and before their selection for a presidency. Such a moment provided fertile opportunity for the ideas "of calling, community service, personal fulfillment, and alignment (of one's own vocation[s] with those of one's spouse and colleagues)" to take firm root among them. But what in their lives, experiences, and purposes made that moment so fertile?

The answer is spread through their stories as told in the interviews. I have reconstructed these stories in this chapter for the purpose of revealing what these deans-become-presidents and their spouses tell us about the distinguishing features of living and thinking vocationally in American academe, in contrast with living and thinking in terms of career and profession. This grounding, helped by the subsequent testimony of other, longer-serving presidents, allows us to attempt, in Chapters Two and Three below, to distinguish the vocational presidency in practice from others that are differently motivated.

Vocational Commitment as a Qualification for the Presidency

A provost with an impressive record of service to a particular tradition in Catholic higher education came to the program with a strong desire to become a president in that tradition. Even though she was not Catholic, she twice had been a finalist in recent presidential searches by Catholic colleges.

An accomplished academic search specialist whose counsel we offered to that particular seminar suggested that the effort be abandoned. Although a recent papal bull had permitted Catholic institutions to elect non-Catholic presidents, the counselor reckoned from wide experience in the academic leadership market in general, and in that segment of it in particular, that the provost's career would stall if she insisted on holding out for her preference. This counsel certainly was respectful of the provost's talent and intentions but was primarily guided, instead, by the concepts of career that have become prominent among employers and search committees in independent institutions in American higher education.

The advice shook the dean's resolve. Reluctantly, she gave thought to widening and refocusing her search, even though doing so felt like "self-betrayal" as well as embarrassed flight from a tradition to which she had given—and from which she had received—much.

The next day, a facilitator of that seminar who was particularly familiar with, and deeply respectful of, Catholic colleges and universities helped the provost to see, in her pained reaction to the search specialist's prudent advice, that it wasn't the presidency per se that was calling her; it was service to a particular educational tradition. The facilitator considered the dean an attractive candidate for several open presidencies and a very highly qualified one for any that might eventually open in that particular Catholic tradition. Reassured by this second opinion, the dean held onto her original intention and eventually won an especially fitting presidency. She has since led that institution to greater clarity of purpose and deeper commitment to mission, and she has acquired a deeper sense of fulfillment and self-confidence along the way.

The tradition to which the dean was dedicated was neither her natal culture nor the one she eventually chose as her religious home. She traces her embrace of it to other, earlier elements of her identity. It was upon these elements and the life and work to which they seemed to point that she and her spouse (who works outside of academe) focused their joint attention both before and during their participation in the Presidential Vocation and Institutional Mission Program. They found the exercise, played out in the matrix of formal, collegial, and marital conversation that extended the reach and depth of the seminar inquiry into their personal lives, mutually rewarding.

Through that exercise, they discovered in their separate biographies a common array of service and leadership obligations, though to very different industries and occupations. This discovery strengthened what already marked their very empathic relationship, namely, something that might be called "inter-vocational cordiality." We saw other examples of this cordiality among both prospective and sitting presidents and their spouses. Each spouse was sympathetic to the calling of the other, and each embraced the discernment and pursuit of their respective vocations as a shared responsibility.

Their interview suggested a notable idea about the nature of calling, an idea echoed in other interviews, more often of sitting presidents than prospective presidents. The suggestion was that the tradition to which the dean had come as a stranger and later to which she had become committed had somehow called *her* into *its* service! She and her spouse understand her presidential leadership to her college as compensation for all that the tradition has given her. They also see it as service to those as yet unknown whom her leadership eventually will benefit.

Program Facilitation of Vocational Discernment among Prospective Presidents

Although three or four other deans and vice presidents also received wise and distinctively vocational counsel from the program in securing fitting presidencies, this outcome was not the principal measure of the program's success. Nor was it that 25–30 percent of the sixty-five provosts, deans, and other academic executives who participated in it as prospective presidents have since become presidents. This result—which was actually achieved—should not have been surprising. High leadership turnover continues to plague American academe. Postings abound. Further, every "prospective" (as we called them) in the program had been nominated to it by a sitting president familiar with and impressed by their work. In short, the program prospectives constituted a rarefied mixture of proven executive competence, presidential promise, and declared interest either in seeking a presidency or seriously wondering if they should. It is not at all clear that the "graduation" of these prospectives from the Presidential Vocation and Institutional Mission Program had any bearing, one way or the other, on their success in winning a presidency.

What is clear, however, is that all eighteen prospectives interviewed— thirteen of whom have won presidencies, three of whom continue to try, and two who don't now want a presidency—say that the program changed the nature and focus of their ambition and narrowed the range of colleges and universities whose employment they would accept.

The factor that more than any other facilitated such deep and abiding personal reorientation was the full inclusion of spouses in the inquiry. The first interview question, "What first seized your interest in the inquiry?" was almost always answered by what one prospective described as "the equal honor and respect" paid by the program to the participation of spouses. This full inclusion of spouses was perhaps the chief attraction of the program. It turned out to enrich the inquiry to an extent far surpassing our expectations because it brought into the seminars one of the key conditions of vocational discernment: friendship.

"I applied to the program," said one dean, "in order to do what my husband and I never found time for at home, namely, to talk with each other about our particular dreams and to see how they fit together." Another said he signed up when he realized that the program was not "just another professional development workshop" in which one is coun- seled on when and how to reach for a presidency. Since he wondered *whether* to reach for a presidency, rather than *when*, he "jumped" at the chance to think this through with his wife beside him.

It turned out that his wife was ready to take full advantage of her inclusion. She described herself as "floundering" when she joined the seminar, "wondering what my role would be when (not if) he became a president. I supported him but wanted to be something more than 'the wife.' I'd been trying to find my personal role. What I needed was to be comfortable with myself."

A dean from a college that had used a grant it received from the Lilly Endowment's Programs for the Theological Exploration of Vocation (PTEV) to draw its faculty and staff into vocational discernment wanted a similar opportunity for himself and his wife. They treasured the remoteness of the program's retreat site because it allowed them three days uninterrupted by the demands of work and family to consider whether their lives and occupations were in service to or at odds with their callings.

Another dean whose academic spouse had followed her to three different colleges brought him to the program in order to win his acceptance of her ambition for a presidency. The fact that the program nurtured spouses as much as prospective presidents opened an exciting prospect to them—that the eventual decision to accept a particular presidency might be made collaboratively and might turn out to be mutually fulfilling.

One couple from an evangelical Christian college, fluent in the theological language of vocation, brought three questions to the program: "Are we called to the vocation of president? Are we fit for that call? How do we find the right place in which to follow the call?" Although they proposed to answer the first two questions themselves, they report that much of their reflection was inspired by the seminar inquiry. They openly sought the counsel of their seminar colleagues to help them answer the third.

Several spouses came to the program to learn for the first time why and to what degree their aspiring mates wanted to be presidents and discovered some interesting things about their own inclinations. They also wanted to know in advance how their lives would change with the arrival of a presidency. All of them arrived with a desire to learn how they might best help their prospective presidents to attain and then to manage a presidency.

Yet another dean and his wife used the seminar principally to develop a profile of the institution that best matched their talents, tastes, and needs. A facilitator noticed that this profile, which had appeared in preliminary form in his application to the program, mirrored the requirements of a position recently advertised. She pointed this out to the couple, and he was selected by that institution within the year. In the interview, he described the college that chose him as a "dead ringer" for the one his wife and he had imagined.

The very few prospectives who came to the program alone relied relatively heavily upon self-reflective conversation with program facilitators for discernment; but they shared equitably with their married colleagues in the exchange of testimonials in both the formal and extra-curricular conversations of the inquiry.

Variations in Discernment among Prospectives and Spouses

These vignettes suggest that the spouses of the prospectives were, in general, less clear about their own aspirations than were the prospectives about theirs. This uncertainty was a great gift to the program. It contributed to something of an alliance that formed in each seminar between the spouses, on the one hand, and the uncommitted prospectives—those who came to the program wondering whether they should seek a presidency or not—on the other. This informal alliance helped us fend off the incessant request for practical advice in landing and managing a presidency—a request commonly voiced by prospectives who not only knew that they wanted a presidency but just what presidency they most preferred. Ultimately, this alliance secured the hospitable atmosphere for vocational discernment that was the first objective of the program.

In reading the reflections on vocation submitted by nominees to the Presidential Vocation and Institutional Mission Program, it was often difficult to distinguish between prospectives who simply wanted a presidency from those who desired a presidency so long as it would make effective use of their talents in a good cause. Ironically, what compounded this difficulty is the growing credibility of vocational language and thinking in academe. Vocation is rightly described as a "calling." In the secular academy, this means something audible only to the one who is called. It's very hard to know whether he or she who claims to be "called" is pursuing a preference, an illusion, or a responsibility. In fact, there is now no better way in colleges and universities to camouflage naked ambition—for power, for prestige, for higher income—than to claim one feels "called" to the work one seeks. Such ambitions have long been rife in the academy but have been only rarely admitted; they are associated among independent undergraduate liberal arts colleges in particular with "corporate life" or—more dismissively—with "capitalism." This is surely one reason why the academy is vocation's largest industrial convert. As an accomplished American sociologist observed during a consultancy about the methodology and argument of this book, "The claim of many academics to the mantle of vocation is mere elocution!"

One of the prospectives, who entered the deliberation skeptical of the program's utility but completed it full of gratitude for its contributions to his own discernment, remembered an early exchange in his seminar. "We were discussing stories of great vocational achievement, even martyrdom. We already felt comfortable enough with each other that two or three said openly that they were ready to become a president so that they could do something significant and were just waiting for God to call them. And I was astonished that hearing a voice might really be a reason for doing something. And I spoke up, saying, 'I don't hear voices; I hear noise.' But I was confident enough about my own skills that

I thought I could be a president. I remember saying, 'Is it okay to just be ambitious? You know, ambitious in its really simple sense?' I've done these things: successful classroom teaching, publishing, addressing large audiences after which I heard remarks like, 'Wow! That was really smart!' (You know that academics really love that stuff!) So I just used the word 'ambitious,' and I said, 'I just want to be a president. Is it okay if I stay in the seminar?' And that teased out a few other similar confessions."

By requiring a testimonial on vocation from applicants to the Presidential and Institutional Mission Program, we were guaranteed significant enrollment of "vocationists"—by their own lights—in every seminar. (The confessing skeptic above was rare among us.) Only when they actually arrived and entered into the inquiry in the presence of their peers and facilitators were we really able to distinguish those who were simply ambitious from those who were interested in discerning their callings.

Two of the uncertain deans claimed in the interviews that the professional development options available in academe are increasingly "corporate" in their presumptions. These programs conceive of college and university administration as what one called a "progression of academic attainment." Those programs, he said, "don't look at you, at *your* purposes, and they don't ask whether the step they say is next in this progression is the right one for you. The fact that it is 'next' is what makes it 'right.'" "And if you don't take that next step when it's time," said another, "you're asked, 'Where did you fail? Where did you plateau?'" Both agreed that such programs were born in the corporate world and are guided by career rather than vocational thinking.

Another prospective who was intent upon obtaining a presidency but only where he could identify with the institution's mission noticed that several members of his particular seminar lost interest in the presidency in the course of the seminar inquiry. A couple of these people, he thought, were unhappy in their current positions and eventually not only refused to try for a presidency but stepped off what he called "the career ladder" altogether.

The Conflation of Vocation and Work

Other aspiring presidents balked at our insistence on a program axiom that one's vocation may point to one's occupation but is not identical with it. They had carefully constructed impressive records of increasing responsibility and rank in a particular institution or family of institutions. Their strategy was to make of that record a ladder to a presidency—and, in a couple of cases, to a particular presidency.

In fact, these deans were busy forging careers. The record of experience around which they had fashioned their resumes functioned for these careers as did "discernment" and "calling" for vocations, and "president" was their next and ultimate station stop. By mustering support for open-mindedness and uncertainty, we led at least one of these experience-bound deans away from career and toward vocation. We secured the first and critical part of the task by driving home one small point: if any of us were to identify our job as our vocation, we would thereafter be unable to assess the vocational propriety of any new work we might happen to take up. Knowing whether our work is the right thing for us to be doing depends upon keeping some separation between vocation and job.

Another limitation of conflating vocation and job is that it confines the range of one's appropriate work to the current employing institution or, perhaps, to a small group of closely associated institutions. And it confines it to the current rank or position and, of course, to those positions often considered "next" in higher education's ladder of ascent. Hence, ambition in the service of career is restricted to proximate and familiar positions to which promotion would mark waypoints on an ascending path in the organizational landscape that is expected to end simply "closer to the top." When careers take shape at the behest of ambition, shrewd calculation guides the choice of which opportunities to pursue. On the other hand, vocations, once discerned, open a richer array of opportunity each of which offers fulfillment in the place of ascent—a sense of one's own place in one or several human communities rather than an ascendancy of self above or beyond community.

One whose allegiance is exclusively to career is more likely to move from job to job, each chosen on the supposition that it is an advance upon the last. The vocationist moves from one job to another on the supposition that each that seems fitting is evidence that there exists in the world of opportunity a "place" somehow reserved for and calling out to oneself. Vocation prompts the pilgrim to look for a distinctive path—even among those that are not particularly beckoning—the full itinerary of which may not be visible except in retrospect.

For several of the deans nominated to the Presidential Vocation and Institutional Mission Program as "prospective presidents," a particular presidency was the exclusive object of their ambition. For them, this specific ambition became an imprisoning as well as inevitable prospect. No mistake is more common in the effort to discern one's calling in contemporary American academe—and none is harder to avoid—than this conflation of vocation and work, calling and experience. And none is as easily co-opted under the elastic tent of popular vocationism. Allowing this conflation of vocation and work to go unchallenged would have hampered the program's search for the appropriate alignment of personal vocation with institutional mission. Instead of tacit acceptance of the conditions that normally lead "experienced" deans to the presidency, the program encouraged probing inquiry into the question: What is the nature of the college or university in which I might make an effective and fulfilled president?

Two of the program prospectives were eventually offered presidencies for which they had long and loyally waited. In both cases, the wheels of vocational growth had slowed to a crawl. They got going again only after the presidencies turned out to be hard to secure and perform once obtained. These difficulties and many others were unexpected because the new presidents' ambitions had been focused exclusively upon gaining the presidency and not on his or her role once there. Waiting for an internal appointment to such a position can block a reflective, confessional, or even prayerful deliberation out of which discernment emerges. Even when the dream of being appointed is fulfilled, the waiting can leave few if any growth marks on the candidate's self-consciousness.

The Role of Friendship in Vocational Discernment

The college or university presidency is not necessarily more vocational than other employment. What makes the position a vocational choice, a career advancement, or a professional achievement—is the president and his or her orientation to the position.

One prospective who is now a president explained why he thought a few of the members of his seminar lost interest in the presidency during the inquiry. "I thought there was something really powerful going on there," he said. "These people were really wrestling with their sense of calling, and several of them were noticing that the purpose they were serving in their current work was neither satisfying to them nor attuned to their college's mission." He thought they backed away from the presidency in light of this realization in order to reconsider the ground of their own engagement in independent higher education. Watching this develop, he said, "made me doubly attentive to the 'fit' between me and my work."

A provost with an eight-year tenure came to the seminar to confront—with his wife's help—his "intense sense of isolation and loneliness" in his work. "I think what intrigued me initially about the program was the opportunity to think through my own values and belief system to see what they were calling me to do. I supposed that my wife and I would do this alone. But what I found were people who hardly knew each other talking openly about really substantive, personal—not just learned or "intellectual"—things. They were wondering about their particular values and talents (rather than announcing and defending their beliefs) and how to apply them in higher education in service to the larger world. That really fired my imagination, and with my wife's help, I got off my intellectual high horse and got back to myself—with both her and their help—to find my path."

These testimonials suggest that there is something profoundly relational about vocational discernment. A skeptic, who participated in the seminar without the company of his spouse, was possessed of a rare reflectivity that allowed him to exploit his remarkable literacy for the sake of his own clearer discernment. He seemed to rely on the seminar sessions exclusively to inspire his own thinking. Others pointed far more often to marital or informal conversation, and remembered what they heard from spouse or friend at least as clearly as their own verbal contributions.

One of the deans who entered the program uncertain about his interest in a presidency discovered an unacknowledged fascination with the traditions and culture of the institution that had long employed him. This discovery not only squelched his meager ambition for a presidency; it sent him back to his deanship with a commitment to advance still further reforms on which he had collaborated with his president to integrate the humanities with undergraduate professional studies. He brought back to his work certain biases the seminar had suggested as particularly vocational in an academic setting. He had come to understand that sampling the wide array of subjects offered in the institution's curriculum did not at all equal the "general education" achieved by the earlier systematic linking of key subjects by an ascending order of complexity.

Although he immediately withdrew from the presidential search scene, he reentered it two years later on the strength of his newly found confidence in the purpose and effectiveness of his work, both of which he associated with vocational discernment. He applied one clear condition to his reentry: he would accept appointment only to an institution committed to the educational principles he was now serving. He has said that a part of him hopes that no such presidency comes knocking. But if it does, he will be compelled by what he takes to be the vocational ethic to accept the call.

His spouse reported during the seminar (and remembered during the interview) an incident that suggested the vital importance of confessional conversation in catalyzing the conversion of career or profession into vocation. After a particularly exciting day of seminar deliberation that triggered an extensive informal confessional conversation with two other couples in the program, she had said to him, "I'd like to know better and talk more with that man who had such interesting things to say this afternoon!" "And who was that?" asked the dean. "You!" said the spouse. "You were talking openly today about things important to both of us but which we have never shared before. I loved it!"

Self-Doubt and Vocational Discernment

This spouse explained that she had sensed emerging from him a new willingness to share the deepest concerns of his work with her, instead of treating the ideas as his own or leaving them at the office. She began to hear from him a confession of self-doubt that even his apparently successful deanship might be beyond his competence, to say nothing of a presidency. They each described the confession of this doubt as "liberating"—and they clearly meant liberation *from* the fear as well as *to* a comparatively unrestrained engagement in life and work. The fact that this breakthrough occurred, for them and several others, outside of the formal discussions helps to explain why the informal atmosphere that developed in each program seminar has been identified regularly as the greatest program contribution to participants' vocational discernment.

Among academics, these liberating conversations about self-doubt are not only limited by the pace and preoccupations of workaday life, especially in dual-career homes, but also by the culture that honors knowledge and the telling of it rather than wonder and the celebration of it. As I discovered during the interviews and in the one-on-one seminar consultations that Anne Frame and I conducted with members of our "permanent groups," the matters that engender the self-doubt typical among academics are of two sorts. One concerns career and is adjudicated by institutions. The other concerns profession and is adjudicated by the academic enterprise. In the case of the first, the speed of one's advancement in rank might have been affected by one's reputation as a teacher and campus citizen among colleagues, students, and administrators. In the case of the second, one's standing might be affected by the amount, orthodoxy, and defense of one's scholarship as perceived and judged by peers and mentors in one's field of study.

In either case, the vocationist needs friends to whom truth can be told and from whom it can be heard on such questions as, "How do I seem to be doing? How am I truly doing? Am I doing the right work, and how do I—or you—know?"

The culture on the campuses of America's independent colleges and universities generally does not invite the pursuit of such questions, to say nothing of the confession and exploration of disappointment with one's performance or achievements. According to the accounts of presidents in the Presidential Vocation and Institutional Mission Program, this culture doesn't readily supply close friends—at least to senior administrators. Until these questions and any disappointments the answers to them entail are freely confessed to a true and caring friend or perhaps to one's god or both, these subjects of silence or avoidance make their presence known by blocking the reflective processes necessary for clear discernment.

One prospective reported that he and his spouse came to the program to escape the strain of managing the juxtapositions of his deanship, his spouse's professional life and young motherhood, and his doctoral study. Although they left the children, the work, and the dissertation behind, they found they could not escape the dilemma. (As another prospective said, "You can't pursue vocation in a vacuum.") In this case, it was the spouse rather than the prospective who brought the issue of self-doubt into the marital conversation.

Her life was being pushed away from professional independence and toward dependence and domesticity by the way his rising promise in the academy increasingly drew on their resources. In the current circumstance and, even more, in the prospect of his eventual presidency, it was the loss of identity that she felt that first precipitated his confession of guilt regarding this inequity. This admission led them back to the deeper question: was he pursuing a calling that promised a sense of fulfillment or was he trying to satisfy the expectations of his sponsors and admirers? The doubt he confessed at this point was that the sponsors and admirers, including his wife, overestimated him. This doubt, they concluded, would probably never be laid to rest; her reassurance, for example, was compromised by a mutually acknowledged conflict of interest. And it was their acceptance of self-doubt that sent them back, collaboratively, to the fundamental vocational question: were they moving, independently yet in association, more and more fully into a life of service in which they could invest their particular gifts with real abandon and high self-confidence, or were they marching (however much in step) to a reputational drum? Shel Silverstein's *The Missing Piece Meets the Big O* suggests the distinction between these two paths.[1]

Another couple came to the program wondering how to balance equitably the demands of their separate careers. They, too, wondered whether each was compromising the happiness of the other by taking more from the marriage than their due. The prospective had been powerfully impressed by Parker Palmer's report, in his principal book on

---

1. Shel Silverstein, *The Missing Piece Meets the Big O* (New York: Harper & Row, 1981).

vocation, that he had learned through a Quaker "clearness committee" his real motivation for wanting to become a college president—so that he could see "my picture in the paper with the word *president* under it."[2] Hence, as the formal seminar inquiry moved from the distinction between career and vocation, ambition and calling, to friendship as the crucial condition of discernment, this couple founded their own clearness committee to answer the question: "Why are we both working so hard?"

They found their answer to this question in the narrative of their journeys in the academy. Upon reflection, they discovered that they each had come into the world of education by seizing upon an "opportunity" and had risen to their current positions and expectations by a continuing stream of "chances," each of which presented risks that seemed "worth taking" at the time. This reflection led each to a deeper respect for the interests and talents of the other—and thus to what I earlier called "inter-vocational cordiality." They concluded, as the interview made clear, that what explained their particular vocations were the narrative shapes of their occupational journeys. The landmarks for each of those journeys consisted of "opportunities" on which they took "a chance" from which emerged widened interests and capabilities. Those widened interests and capabilities redefined, in turn, what they would next see as "opportunity" and altered their calculus of risk and reward. For them, the greatest benefit of the program was the confidence that each was on an "appropriate" path and that the paths "concurred" but didn't merge.

A third dual-career couple, also with young children, came to the seminar to talk about the "long-term logistics" of their marriage that were constantly supplanted even on their carefully planned "evenings out" by "short-term" considerations: With whose family will we spend Thanksgiving and Christmas? What shall we do about an aging parent?

---

2. Parker J. Palmer, *Let Your Life Speak: Listening for the Voice of Vocation* (San Francisco: Jossey-Bass, 1999), 46.

Where shall we take the kids for vacation this year? For them, the program "created the space and time" for the long-term matters. "We had great conversations when we were hiking, when we were in the seminar room, when we were just walking on the property or sitting by the fire." And they befriended a similarly situated couple with whom they compared notes.

For the spouse of the prospective, in this case, these marital and social conversations, made "explicit the way I think, not about 'her' vocation or 'my' vocation, but about how I need to support her in her vocation and how I accept the costs of that support." Although the two shared the same field of study, his occupational opportunities had once included frequent international travel to provide consulting services. In the place of these, he had consciously narrowed his work to his employer's classrooms. "The most important thinking that came out of the program for me was not about how I fit into the effort to transform the institution that she was leading but how I might support her in doing that."

His spouse explained that this deliberation between them "made my vocation our vocation. That doesn't mean that he agrees with every piece of my work or that all of the sacrifices are his, but he really adopted my presidency as *ours*—and he carries through to the degree that he can do it within his career." They both illustrated this agreement with vignettes in which he edited drafts of her speeches, offered an occasional lecture at the college, and patiently accepted briefings about donors with whom they were to meet.

A fourth couple came to the program because it was sponsored by "the first professional organization to recognize that a person's spouse is an essential part of both being a president and thinking about becoming one." This couple quickly realized that most of their colleagues possessed "a specific idea of career advancement and had every intention of seeking a presidency." Both he and his spouse, a craft artist, were among those who ranged "along the continuum from skeptical" about reaching for a presidency at all to wondering whether there were opportunities especially attuned to their particular capabilities. They left with far more confidence in their readiness for a presidency than when they arrived because "we had the opportunity to engage with this array of people who were considering the same prospect but from a far wider circle of institutions than we normally experienced."

The Balanced versus the Centered Life

Two of the prospective couples interviewed, both from an early seminar and in a presidency for about three years, expressed deep gratitude to one of the program facilitators, Steve Jennings, a three-time president and facilitator in the first seminar for prospectives in 2005. He had brought a vocational-discernment template called a "shield" to the seminar. It asked the user to rank lifestyle preferences in several categories such as occupation, avocation, and undirected leisure. These couples learned from using the shield that they shared a broad array of values and practices, and this suggested that they very well might pursue separate vocations within a marriage that was "centered." Furthermore, it suggested that there may be room for putting two vocations into service to each other rather than making one the servant of the other or radically separating them.

These marriages were experienced in "balancing" dual-career demands. What vocation brought to them were two things: an acceptance of the differences as evidence of vocational integrity for each partner and the possibility that the presidency might be shared without resulting in the loss of either partner's vocation. In both cases, what had been a compromise for each—one change of venue driven by one partner, and the next by the other—became a partnership for the full liberation of the vocational fervor of each.

For one couple, the presidency itself became the centering factor that they sought but couldn't find earlier. Even when her commitment to the presidency had guided their movements from institution to institution, both prospective and spouse had been living with neither balance nor center. Hers had been the "higher" ambition; he had "adapted" to the mobility her ambition required of both. She therefore had good reason to bring him and her worry about the imbalance—the fundamental inequity in this pattern—to the program.

But the actual arrival of the presidency, after the seminar and before the interview, changed the nature and challenge of their relationship. Although it meant, once again, a job search for him—which was successful, as the earlier ones had been—the huge absorption of her energies by the position about which she had so long dreamed brought into their relationship all of the characteristics of a "final destination." In a sense, her job took the place of her ambition as the guiding force in their shared life, and the question of dual-career equity was replaced by a simpler, more compelling question: how can we assemble the human resources needed for this work from within the relationship? Hence, the presidency itself—since it couldn't really be escaped, even by the most vigorous alternative spousal career—became the joint work of the couple. This couple saw their resignation to the absorbing power of the presidency as a transformation from gender equity (to which they were deeply dedicated) to vocational equity. And the imperial character of the presidency made it possible for them to quietly acknowledge another unsettling facet of "inter-vocational cordiality," namely, that even though each of us may have his or her calling, some lives are, in fact, more vocational—more serviceable to public or community interests—than others.

From Discernment of Vocation to the Pursuit of Vocation

Now the question of balance versus centeredness took on new meaning. If vocation is to continue to characterize the presidency once gained, as it characterized the presidency once sought, it must move to a new level. Discernment is now needed, not for the work and life to which one is called, but for the purpose that the work serves. Without a compelling answer to this new question—or without a serious effort to answer it—vocation may be excused and replaced with some other kind of thinking pertaining to management, administration, or institutional maintenance.

It is conceivable, but only barely, that the prospect of contentment might attract some to the presidency. To some harried by corporate life in a big city the traditional college presidency of long tenure on a bucolic, small-town campus seems comfortable, quiet, prestigious, and very appealing. But vocationists eventually realize that the success of their work and their own sense of fulfillment depend upon a vitality that comes from the dialectic between self and duty. And so they ultimately seem to stop yearning for a contentment that many presume might accompany a perfectly cohesive life. They also seem to shun managerial, administrative, and maintenance presidencies but seem prone to embrace instead a restless search for new projects of repair, initiation, or renewal.

Well after her presidency did, in fact, become the joint work of the dual-career couple who came to the seminar looking for vocational equity, I asked the president, "Is your vitality flagging or rising?" "It would depend literally on the day you ask me," she said. "There are days when I am high on the possibilities and there are other days when someone's taken the school to court because they were not 'respected,' and the budget's in the toilet because we lost 23 percent of the endowment and I have to lay off a secretary. I mean there are days when you think, 'I'm not cut out for this! There's not enough joy in it and joy has got to be an element.' And there are other days where someone will say, 'I believe in what you're doing and here's a million dollars! Keep it up!' On those days, the joy is high because the money makes the imagined possible. I've heard presidents say that they absolutely love it—all the time. Not me. It depends on the day you ask me."

Here was a president in need of an organizing purpose of which she would be both author and executor, something more reliable than sporadic bursts of philanthropy to fend off the exhaustion of trying to accommodate the myriad and competing interests of the college's constituencies. Another of her statements indicates that she knew this and was well along in developing such a purpose. When I asked her what work remained ahead in her presidency, she said: "I'd like to be a president centered in my job, not at all interested in leaving it, excited at the prospect of seeing the institution independent but immersed in its own qualities and characteristics—which I've helped it find. Of course, if you ask your question of presidents casually, they'll report that they're exhausted and all that. But, you know, some of them are feeling fulfilled, because they're making a difference for a worthy cause."

The constant sharpening of discernment demanded by the commitment to make the presidency vocational—as distinguished from the career planning required to obtain the presidency—requires a special kind of courage. While it encompasses the courage to confess self-doubt, it goes beyond it. Indeed, I think it consists in a risk-taking opportunism—the sort of thing described above by the prospective and spouse who created occupational narratives as the source of their callings. That sort of opportunism consists in exploring initiatives that appear as both important and useful but which are beyond the experience, and maybe, therefore, the competence of their initiators.

Such opportunism and experimentalism is allegedly difficult for one group that is generally supposed to be well represented among college and university presidents, namely, the highly promising and especially capable. Po Bronson and Ashley Merryman, in *Nurture Shock: New Thinking about Children*, report that those taught to think of themselves as gifted often divide the world of human activity into things they are good at and things they are not good at. Then, they refuse even to attempt the latter.[3]

---

3. Po Bronson and Ashley Merryman, *Nurture Shock: New Thinking about Children* (New York: Twelve, 2009), 11–12.

But the notably vocational prospectives who became presidents appeared frequently to go beyond their experience on behalf of initiatives that promised better health and welfare to the college or university. These presidents seemed to know that doing so does not, of itself, constitute vocational discernment. They agree, however, that this activity is requisite for those who mean to make their presidencies vocational. Urging the institution to consider new policies or enterprises widens the range both of one's competence (even if it sometimes adds to the "not good at" list) and of one's social engagement. It contributes to the development of a distinctive kind of self-confidence that marks the vocational presidency.

Creative vs. Vocational Leadership

This self-confidence neither leads to nor derives from what is usually thought of as "creative leadership." I asked a new president who had participated in the program as a prospective to respond to the proposition that presidential leadership is "creative."

> I would say that there are very few things that I, as president, create. One thinks that there's a lot of power in the presidency but there is much more power in empowering. I have come up with very little on my own, but there's a whole lot that a group of us has done together. In every area, it's a different group of "us." Sometimes, I'm not even involved in the "us." I've allowed it to happen or helped foster it, but I had nothing to do with the initiative. I really think that if you want satisfaction from your job in terms of being able to point to the difference that you individually make, the college presidency is not necessarily the job for you.

Another new president suggested that the source of the creativity that emerges in a vocational presidency lies in the institution itself,

41

conceived as a tradition or—better still—a "living" tradition. I asked him to describe vocational presidential leadership. "I think it is a kind of incarnational leadership," he said. "You become a part of it rather than standing outside of it, and you are as affected as you are affecting." When I asked for an illustration, he said: "The key notion of vocation—and of a college conceived of as vocational—is the idea of 'becoming.' If you quit becoming, you quit living." And how, I asked does that apply to a college? "No living organism goes unchanged," he said, "and sometimes the faculties of small, financially sound colleges contradict their liberal political leanings and try to stop all institutional change, all development, all evolution, thinking that there's nothing left to build or alter—that it's finished." I then asked, "What can you do as a new president—parachuted in from some entirely different tradition—about that conservatism?" "I think it's particularly important to tell the institution's story—with its heroes who, at certain key points in its history, put the college above self—especially when you're coming from outside. That's part of how you earn your stripes, and people begin to say, 'Okay! He or she is becoming one of us—beginning to understand who we are and how we came to be.'" That, we agreed, is where the peculiar authority of the vocational presidency is born.

The current shortage of qualified presidential candidates has forced some sectarian and denominational colleges to elect presidents from outside their traditions. This infusion of "outsiders" is bringing "new blood" into these traditions, and we encountered several examples of this phenomenon among the thirteen new presidents interviewed for this book. Because they lack a qualifying birthright, these émigrés must actually demonstrate (rather than merely stipulate) their understanding of and sympathy for the relevant tradition. While their empathy with the tradition does not guarantee that they are better citizens than those native to it, they regularly and publicly will have to present their credentials. This finding runs counter to the central argument of Father James

Tunstead Burtchaell's *Dying of the Light: The Disengagement of Colleges and Universities from Their Christian Churches*. In the final chapter, he writes: "In many of these stories [of dying light] the critical turn away from Christian accountability was taken under the clear initiative of a single president."[4] Presidential Vocation and Institutional Mission Program participants who were outsiders to such traditions, however, usually enlivened those traditions. Presidents, in fact, who mine their adopted traditions for the sake of institutional envisioning proved to be much more likely to become and remain vocational than those selected from within.

The spouse of another new president, a professional in her own right whose engagement in the presidency led her to join several community service organizations in the environs of the college, drew a parallel between a "creative" president and a volunteer trustee who comes to meetings four times a year with his or her own view of how the place should be run. "Neither of these is guided by the larger entity. Each has his or her own agenda."

One of the nonprofits she joined had acquired a board that regularly failed to assemble a quorum. When it did, the trustees would come at the issue of the moment from so many angles that they were unable to act. By contrast, she continued, "Now, they've set up a trustee recruitment process to determine if candidates understand the organization, agree with its purpose, want to be a board member, and can articulate why the organization should elect them."

Her husband added that a president who is trying to find the voice of a college needs the board to validate the search, not to identify the voice or what it says. He agreed with his wife that "it's exhausting to listen to someone who knows everything"—as board members sometimes do.

---

4. James Tunstead Burtchaell, *Dying of the Light: The Disengagement of Colleges and Universities from Their Christian Churches* (Grand Rapids, Mich.: Eerdmans, 1998), 826.

"Nevertheless, faculties want to know what the president thinks," he said. "They really don't want to deliberate with the president about who the college really is and what they should, together, do for it. Colleges need vocational presidents," he said, "but they don't think so; they think they want creative visionaries."

Others confirm that the most frequently asked question of candidates for a college or university presidency is, "What vision will you bring to us here at Old Siwash?" Most of the prospectives who experienced the Presidential Vocation and Institutional Mission Program claim that they answered this question by decrying any vision for Old Siwash—except that of Old Siwash itself.

Vocational Humility

Once a vocational president gets wind of the voice that speaks best of a college's character and longing, his or her job is to get and stay in dialogue with it. That dialogue serves two purposes: it lifts and clarifies the voice, and it sustains the authority of the initiatives that are intended to approximate its ambition. Both functions of the dialogue reduce the importance of the president's own persona.

One of the prospectives who obtained a presidency early in the history of the program put it this way: "I knew that my job as president was to step back at a speed that matched that with which I put the vision forward." When I asked him what satisfaction he drew from deliberately reducing his role, he answered: "I entered this world of learning—or, at least, I stayed in it—to associate with great minds and great ideas. The institutional self-image that we are elaborating and extending at my college has been drawn together from the seminal work of a remarkable collection of such minds."

A day before the interview, he had used this observation to explain to his wife why he wasn't hurt by the public relations department's failure to give him proper credit for a celebrated philanthropic windfall:

"I am here to diminish myself on behalf of the college." It is significant that his college had, some years earlier, abandoned its sectarian identity to widen its admissions appeal. In the president's view, this reform (of which he heartily approved) increased the college's need of envisioning and of a vocational president to facilitate the process.

Somewhat surprisingly, the personality or character indicator that most reliably marked the vocationism of the presidential prospectives—and, as later chapters will claim, also of the sitting presidents—is humility. This humility lies near the root of the deep self-reflection that characterizes the discernment process among vocationists. In every venue of the program, whether in seminar deliberation, one-on-one consultations with facilitators, or informal marital or personal conversation, they dove farther than their few self-certain colleagues into an investigation of their own motives and were more realistic in their appraisal of the costs and rewards of vocational living than were their prouder peers. They were, therefore, more alert to their need of support in managing the strain and potential exhaustion of what we came to call the "burden" of vocation than either those who said they were following divine directive or those who simply "knew what they wanted." The humility implicit in the alignment of their vocational commitment with the principal themes of the institution they served seemed to free them for the performance of their work without the restraining effects of self-doubt.

Nothing in these observations about humility denies ambition its role in vocational living. However, the ambition that is consistent with vocation consciously *serves* vocation. To do one's duty—excellently, on time, and to loud applause from the narrow audience entrusted by the vocationist with the right of judgment—is the measure of a well-lived life of service. In a "successful career," on the other hand, excellence is measured by the achievement of rank rather than by the amount and quality of the service rendered along the way. The audience that

45

applauds the accomplishments of career may very well include envious and defeated rivals as well as appreciative peers. Indeed, it will almost certainly appreciate "accomplishment" more than personal fulfillment and duty done.

Converting the Presidency from Profession to Vocation

Young Americans have been told for years that to reach the heights in American society they will need a good supply of raw ambition and an admission ticket issued by an independent third party. Ambition is universally viewed in terms of competitiveness. The admission ticket is a license to practice in one of the several professions serving society. In the case of American academe, the profession that supplies the training and grants the ticket is the professoriate.

But in all the world, the professoriate is probably the profession most embarrassed by ambition. And so ambition takes for members of the faculty a stridently modest form. This doesn't banish ambition from the academy but it bends it more often toward professional achievements— one's publication record, one's standing in one's field of study, sometimes the sharpness of one's repartee at professional meetings—than toward respect from administrators, a reputation for effective teaching, or wise counsel.

Hence, two peaks stand above the ambitious academic: full or distinguished professor and president. For faculty to achieve the presidency—and to this day nearly all who are elected to the presidency started out as instructors—they must make it well up the first peak before leaving it to tackle the second. And this does not sit well with their faculty colleagues; they interpret this peak-switching maneuver as changing sides in a great and continuing contest.

There is no parallel in other industries to the sustained distrust that faculty have for administrators. The tension between line and staff in the corporate world is background noise by comparison. The dean who accepts the designation "prospective president"—which nomination to the vocation-mission program automatically conveyed—is inevitably alienated from, and sometimes even ostracized by, his or her professorial colleagues. This breach has been making both the climb up the second peak and occupation of the presidency particularly challenging ever since faculties gave up management of institutional operations at various points early in the twentieth century.

One of the deans participating in the program was greeted by his faculty colleagues upon his appointment as provost with what has become the standard Star Wars image for the purpose: "Well, congratulations! I hear you've moved to the Dark Side?" In fact, the dean found himself describing the appointment in terms of the Star Wars image, which he admits reflects the suspicion of an irreducible core of senior faculty in teaching colleges that the "dark side" is actually more than merely "the other side."

The consequence of the appointment, for him, was a sudden shunning by some of his departmental colleagues—a reaction that didn't at all occur when he accepted the departmental chair or when he was elected to the presidency of the faculty senate. He also said that his president helped him to see that a provost is "a sympathetic [to the faculty] representative of institutional interests" not the faculty's first line of defense against the "administration." (As president, this former provost maintains traction on key issues with his faculty by "staying current" in his field of study; he does this, he says, by relating his professorial interests directly to his presidential leadership.)

Everyone who participated in the Presidential Vocation and Institutional Mission Program had taken at least the first steps out into the open terrain between these two camps. All had reached the borderlands of the profession of scholar/teachers. Some of them had entered the alumni-development circuit and achieved standing with donors, trustees, and others critical to the academic learning community. Some were endorsed by their colleagues to promote the interests of the professoriate in the faculty senate and began there to think institutionally rather than exclusively in the terms of their profession and constituents.

Without acknowledging it as cause of their restlessness, a good number of prospective presidents began the journey to overcome disappointment in their performance when measured by the standards of success erected by the profession of teacher-scholars. Falling short of professional standards in the academy hurts vocational discernment more than the self-doubt precipitated by career disappointments. Career standards are adjudicated by each college or university. They have to do with the speed of one's advance through the ranks and one's reputation for collegiality. Professional standards, on the other hand, are trans-institutional and therefore much more authoritative. They have to do with the significance of one's published scholarship, one's standing among the acknowledged experts in one's field of study, even the height of one's celebrity status. Never mind that these standards are satisfied by a very small number of the profession's membership. These rarely achieved standards remain capable of frustrating institutional efforts to establish distinctive cultures of civility, excellence in counseling students, and lifelong learning. And they turn the walls of academe into a trap rather than a haven, especially for the middle-aged who haven't met them.

The absence of a confessional in the academic profession to which such disappointments can be acknowledged, and through which forgiveness might flow, consigns the disclosure of academic guilt to the deepest recesses of the personal psyche—and thus to the ministrations of friendship. Whether that guilt can be divulged even there depends upon the strength of one's commitment to honesty; if it is strong enough, the imperfections in one's life can be acknowledged and confessed, and the full employment of one's abilities in service to a commanding communal cause can be undertaken.

In any case, the discernment process that leads from profession to career and from career to calling cannot really begin until full disclosure of disappointment has been made before one's conscience. This seems to have happened in several cases among prospective presidents participating in the Presidential Vocation and Institutional Mission Program. The disclosure, the forgiveness, and the finding of the vocational path were each accomplished by way of friendship.

From Scholarship to Envisioning

The largest group we encountered among both presidents and prospective presidents had migrated from humanities faculties to administration. Members of this group were prone to fascination with the institutional, sectarian, and denominational traditions into which they were born or—yet more intriguing—in which they professed. Their scholarship, sharpened by direct relevance to their own lives and immediate circumstances, made them knowing devotees of Jesuit higher education, for example, or Lutheran higher education, or traditional liberal arts education, or some other distinctive educational philosophy. They did not at all escape the criticism of their colleagues when they moved to the "dark side" of administration, but their readiness to join hands with the constituents of the college that selected them for leadership in search of the institution's vision reduced the chances that they would take up the presidency as administration, management, or maintenance rather than as vocation.

The bridge that carried the bulk of those who joined the program as prospective presidents from profession and career to vocation was made of two critical factors—that vocation is a precise concept that is grasped fully only in the act of applying it directly to one's own life and work, and that the program's full inclusion of spouses created the sociality that enabled this direct and practical application (even for those who came alone to the program). Taken together, these factors kept the inquiry personal and practical rather than academic and abstract. Hence, we saw little if any posturing in seminar sessions on behalf of one's institution or one's professional standing. The interview transcripts are replete with reports that the prescribed readings of the program produced a constant stream of sophisticated but practical ideas that enriched marital conversation and then constituted important elements in the web of lasting friendships among those who came to the program as strangers. Respect for the wonder of the idea of vocation itself, and the availability of remarkable literature to illustrate it, kept the informal deliberations of the program "public" (even when they occurred behind closed doors) rather than entirely personal or purely anecdotal.

Conclusion

My conversations with the prospective presidents and spouses convince me that the success of the Presidential Vocation and Institutional Mission Program depended primarily upon the interplay of a burgeoning sociality among participants. Inspired by an intriguing idea and fed by close attention to the rich literature of vocation, this sociality combined with community, practical intellectual curiosity, and scholarship to elicit the enlightened personal reflection that is at the core of vocational discernment. This formula led most of those who later became presidents and many of the sitting presidents interviewed to embrace vocational discernment as a better guide to right living and satisfying work than either career or profession.

CHAPTER 2

From Administration to Envisioning
Shaping the Vocational Presidency

Fifty sitting presidents of CIC-member colleges and universities participated in groups of fifteen to twenty with their spouses in three seminars of the Presidential Vocation and Institutional Mission Program between 2005 and 2009. They came from a wide variety of institutions and personal circumstances. Literally all of those interviewed for this book say they learned something about themselves, their friends, and their work that returned them to their campuses and occupations with new appreciation of the advantages of vocational thinking in personal life and higher education.

What this new appreciation actually consisted of, and what parts of it the presidents applied in leading their colleges and universities—and how—is the subject of this chapter. We begin with why they came to the program in the first place.

Vocation for Presidents vs. Vocation for Presidencies

Several of the presidents participating in the program had used grants from the Programs for the Theological Exploration of Vocation (PTEV), originally supported by the Lilly Endowment, to plant the seeds of vocational thinking on their campuses—most frequently in co- and extracurricular programs. Now they wanted to try out this thinking for themselves and to see how it might be applied next in the college, perhaps to the core curricular and cultural dimensions of institutional life.

"I was absolutely confident," said one of them in an interview three years after the conclusion of her seminar, "that I was 'called' to my presidency when I was selected for it. But the place turned out to have some pretty serious governance issues and the early days of the presidency were really tough—as many nowadays seem to be." Her strong sense of calling sustained and guided her through this early work. Over the span of about five years, she straightened up operations and led the college into a campus-wide conversation about vocation that she described as "transformational" of institutional culture.

At that point, she said, "I was trying 'to revision' what I thought of as the second half of my presidency: What work was next? How long should I stay here? When should I retire?" That's when the program was announced, and she quickly applied. "So I didn't come to the seminar to *begin* thinking about vocation and its application to my institution. I came to ask: 'What shall I do next with the idea?' And one other question had come into my mind: 'How shall I tend to my vocation after I've retired?'"

Already liberated from the restraining modern suspicion that all human purpose is generated by personal preference and career considerations, she grasped from her experience of the seminar that vocational purposes are generically public and communal rather than private and individualistic. She returned to campus deeply determined to apply vocational thinking directly to the college's curriculum and student-life culture. At her insistence, the school's general education requirement was revised in record time, and a mission-centric "vocational leadership institute" was established. The institute was intended to cultivate among students a "commitment beyond self"—her phrase and the college's synonym for "vocation." (The marketing people found that the word "vocation" had been so compromised by association with "vocational education" that using it would mistake the college as an array of "shop" classes. The institute sought greater collaboration between preprofessional and liberal arts programs, each of which had long turned its back on the other. Conversation with her peers in the seminar reinforced her conviction that neither camp could send serviceable vocationists out into the world without the curricular and pedagogical help of the other).

This capacity of vocational thinking to regenerate a public or civic life for academic executives is exemplified by a president who applied to the program immediately upon noticing that it "invited people to get together and talk about" a subject that was dear to him but largely missing from the higher education conference agenda—namely, the "alignment" of work with self. "I had always felt a powerful need," he said, "to check and see that what I'm doing, what I'm spending time and effort on, is consistent with what I've decided is really important to me, to my life." "They've got to pick me," he thought as he sent off his application to the program. "This is the 'meat and potatoes' of what I've always been interested in!"

From his early teenage years, this president wanted to be a college professor and had been thrilled to discover that he enjoyed it immensely. As a scholar, he had been especially watchful for lives that seemed "meaningless"—lives that were incongruent with purpose. In contrast, he said, "I always wanted to be able to say that what I'm doing doesn't just make life possible, doesn't just pay the bills. It's something that is important to *me;* something through which I can contribute to the world outside—outside of both my work and of myself."

It was the realization that contributing to the world outside of both work and self was the true hallmark of vocation that carried him beyond his commitments to "congruence" and simple "alignment." For example, he drew from the seminar conversations—all of which he described as "wonderful"—confirmation that his own journey from the professoriate through administration to the presidency was in fact vocational. This was good news, in that it was consistent with his congruence principle. But it went beyond this principle by accompanying him in the transition from the professoriate to the presidency, a transition he had neither planned nor expected to make. He took note of this in the interview by noticing, with some surprise, that the presidency was at least as fulfilling to him as the professoriate had been. Indeed, he was beginning to describe his ten-year presidency as bringing the college itself into consonance with its mission, just as living "congruently" had helped him give proper shape to his personal life.

This president's spouse—who has rendered high-profile public service in each of the several communities in which they have lived—"having tried, all my life, to define myself separately from him," found through the seminar a new role for herself in the presidency. Her story sharpened the impression of both that the program had added "public service" to "congruence" as a distinguishing mark of lives well lived. "I had often wished," she said during the interview, "that somebody would give me a little discrete place in this world and say, 'Just straighten this out and make it the best it can be!'" As she listened to her husband describe his presidency in the seminar, she realized, "That's what he's doing! That's what he's got!" Hence, she credited the program with giving her "a real sense of enthusiasm for the presidency and for the mission" her husband had been serving. "That gave me a lot more understanding than seeing him leave at 6:30 A.M. and return at 7:00 or 8:30 P.M., after a ballgame or something. While I remain active in the community, I'm now more involved in the presidency and we have more to share with each other."

Despite this "inter-vocational cordiality" (as noted in Chapter One) that she had discovered in her husband's presidency—and the acknowledged benefits in friendship and mutual appreciation it yielded to both of them—she remained fiercely protective of her own independence. "This idea of vocation has an aggressive quality about it," she said. "The first time I heard the spouse of a president say, 'I don't care how much time it takes or how little family time we have, the presidency is our mission,' I thought, 'No! He's got the job, not me. I've got my own interests, only one of which is my role in the presidency.' Besides," she continued, "our relationship would be shattered if we each were doing something as consuming as a presidency; neither of us would then be available to the other in the way that we have now been made *by* the independence of our respective vocations."

The style and purpose of the leadership imminent—and to some degree eminent—in the work of these two presidents is distinctively "vocational." It rises in the form of accurate self-knowledge from a process of discernment that, in the right hands, becomes a strategy for the articulation and realization of institutional identity. Moreover, this service to institutional identity further distinguishes and enriches vocation.

Vocational vs. "Executive" Leadership in Higher Education

Another kind of leadership was represented in the program by a president who came to consider whether it was time to move to another CEO position, either in higher education or elsewhere. He saw as "pretentious," rather than "imperial," the claims of vocationism made by his peers in the program. He blamed this on the currency in the program of a "religious" concept of vocation. "I would have liked to hear more of the 'servant leader' that businesses prize, and less of the 'great leader' doing God's work in the 'sacred' field of education. Being in education is no more 'special' than being in healthcare, or any other field. If you're passionate about the mission of the institution you lead, regardless of the industry, then you have 'a special calling' there and in that work."

This president had come to higher education from a related field and felt his calling was to executive rank or position rather than into the service of a particular industry or community. "Think of the minister," he said,

> who's had an epiphany and was called to become a minister. And then you find out he was "called" to earn a living. I think all kinds of different things bring us to where we are at any given point in our lives. I'm just a driven person; once I take on a commitment, I see it through. It's my nature. I like the challenge of turning something around, and it so happened that my best recent opportunity was education. But, to be honest, I could have the same drive, the same commitment to mission, the same commitment to success if I were running something else. I believe in all these things we told each other in the program about education—I do!—but, for me, it's not the key driver, wasn't the key driver.

Ironically, this president spoke admiringly of friendship—a critical condition of vocational discernment. "You go through ups and downs in any job," he said. "Whoever goes into positions like a college presidency needs a friend to help handle the stress and to figure out when it's time to try something else." The president seemed to insist that while the useful friend is knowing and caring, that friend's familiarity should be with the president's skills and ambition rather than his or her calling. (His presidency has been judged successful by all accounts, yet the salient question for him to this day is, "When and where shall I reach for a new executive position?")

In contrast, one participant who was about to wind up his presidency brought his spouse to the program so that they could look for signs of their vocational responsibilities in retirement. During the inaugural meetings of the seminar, they happened to share a duplex with a president who had just been selected by a college that had been suffering both financial crisis and frequent leadership turnover. At the end of the first day of the seminar, the retiring couple was thrilled to find the newly elected president and his spouse drawing energy and enthusiasm from their deliberation on the tough work that awaited them on campus. "This young president was called where he was needed and was rising to the challenge by way of a growing sense of the 'fit' between his capabilities and the need."

"Long ago," said the veteran during the interview, "I had wanted to go to two or three other places when I turned, instead, to the place I least preferred but which most seemed to need me. It was a very conscious decision, but in looking back with that young president in my mind I see that the choice wasn't really mine! It was as if the college had made the choice simply by waving its need in front of me! I think that's what happened to that young president, and he was literally embracing, as I had, the opportunity to be of service. I had found a soul mate!"

(Others have argued that such a decision as the veteran reported of himself and alleged to the young president might as easily have been taken out of arrogance. If so, they say, the "mistake" eventually will out. In the cases described here, time has confirmed the vocational character of the decision.)

As he and his wife recounted the journey that had led them to the presidency from which they were retiring, they appeared to be trying to make sense of what they described as a "series of epiphanies" that led them to it. They had gotten far enough along in this effort to have seen in these "signs" evidence of extraordinary congruence between their service instincts, their skills (or "gifts," as they called them), their readiness and aptitude for the work, all on the one hand, and the "needs" of the university, on the other. They articulated this explication of what the program called "alignment" in such language as "God's call," "love of neighbor," "service" to the community, and, at the very end of the list, the sense of fulfillment for having done one's duty.

Running through the very center of this "epic of discernment," as the president called it, was a deep contrast between his and his wife's manifest pleasure in telling the story and the tales of trial and tribulation that constituted it. The university turned out to be in greater need than they had supposed. Confronting this greater need precipitated unforeseen conflict with on-campus constituencies as well as disagreement with trustees. Moderating this conflict and building a new intra-institutional coherence was exhausting and trying work, but it supplied the president and his wife a sense of personal fulfilment. The retirement was not altogether unwelcome on the campus. But the president and his wife were clearly dedicated to the university's welfare and to the success of the new president. The presidency had entailed tough but "wonderful" work, and they were hoping for more like it for an equally worthy purpose in retirement.

The president described the process entailed in his and his wife's "epic of discernment." It was a process, he said,

> in which you try to put yourself into the presence of the Holy Spirit, thus to understand God's will. But that's only half of it. The other half is the accepting. And that's often the harder part. After you've prayed without much effect for understanding, you pray for grace. You pray for the willingness to accept the grace when it comes, because there's a very good chance you really won't want it. I didn't want to come to this presidency, but I found peace enough to do what I didn't want to do and I'm glad I did. This has been a hard but fulfilling enterprise.

He believed that he had been "put" into the presidency by divine directive, and he therefore had to "accept" the employment, that is, rationalize and appropriate to himself the particular responsibilities of that presidency in that institution at that point in time. This president thereby reconciled what may seem irreconcilable in the contrast between vocation and career, namely, being *called* to one's life and work while *choosing* them.

The Imperial Propensities of Presidential Vocationism

A spouse came to the seminar as she had to the presidency—as follower and helpmate. Her husband the president "has always been vocational and mission-driven," she said, "no matter where we were or what he was doing. But it's been hard for me to figure out my vocation. I do so many different things—raise the children, manage our own household. I have my own career, and it has nothing to do with the presidency. So I arrived at the seminar thinking, 'I'm just tagging along here.'"

And then she found another spouse who seemed to be in the same boat—except that this woman had come to view her life, complete with an independent career and variety of domestic roles, gathered in a rough symmetry with her husband's under an overarching "umbrella." The friend explained that the vocations gathered under this umbrella were neither melded together nor crowding each other out. The image helped the self-deprecating spouse to see that her several vocations could actually complement those of her presidential husband, but only if they were both independent of and sympathetic toward his, and vice versa. "It made me feel like I fit better into the seminar. And when we came back to campus, I felt much better about my role in the college as the wife of the president."

Part of this spouse's original dependency can be explained by the nature of the president's vocational commitment. He explained:

> I had always seen my life in academia as vocational and mission-driven. But when I got to the presidency, my vocation and its connection with institutional mission was not shared by the

rest of the community, by the faculty in particular. So, I came to the seminar for affirmation of something I knew intellectually but hadn't yet been able to follow through on as a president—that everything you do comes out of your vocation, out of your inner self.

Indeed, he had sometimes wondered whether vocational life was actually applicable in the college or university presidency. "The complexity at this level, and the various constituencies that you have to deal with" made the work seem impossible. Although the conversations triggered by the seminar readings and presentations argued that vocational presidents could be even more effective than non-vocational ones, he had not yet found that true at the time of the interview a year or so later.

The board had hired him to bring the college back to its founding mission—a purpose to which he was fully responsive. The "drift" that he was to reverse was marked by the development of preprofessional and graduate programs that shared little with the original mission of the college. This "mission drift," as he and the board called it, had given the institution economic health, a fundamentally secular ontology, and a culture split by the original liberal arts core, now secularized, on the one hand, and the new and growing overlay of professional programs, on the other.

The new president realized that it would be disastrous to dismantle the professional programs and difficult to find common ground between them and the liberal arts. It seemed to him, therefore, that the only source of institutional coherence was the founding mission, the revival of which the board had explicitly hired him to accomplish. His critics, at least half of whom were scions of the strong and still-growing professional education programs in the college, saw the president's embrace of the arcane institutional traditions as arbitrary and even capricious. They perceived his actions as a rejection of the university in its modern form. The president found himself repeatedly saying to his critics, "I didn't create the mission; it has always been here. You just haven't been talking about it, and now we really must talk about it. That's why I came here. In fact, that's the only reason I came here!"

An observer familiar with these dynamics thought that this was a case in which the board sold to the new president a college that no longer existed. The "mission drift" had not compromised the college's identity; it had changed it. Had that been acknowledged, the immediate task of the vocational president would have been to gather from the college the threads of accommodation from which a legitimizing vision might be woven. As it was, however, the president's goal was to restore an identity that had been lost somewhere among the accommodations. Hence, the founding vision was no longer registered deeply enough in the consciousness of the place either to hold it together or to provide it with a bridge across which it might make its way into a new era.

This couple's experience of the seminar brought them each to trans-formed roles in the presidency—she with new vocational self-confidence and he with the capacity to "rationalize" and thereby "appropriate" to himself the responsibilities of one who had been placed by providence into the presidency of that particular college at a particular moment in its history.

For a long time, he said, "the frustration of my struggle for the heart and soul of the college has made me more committed to my vocation here." But the depth of the frustration as he acknowledged it in the pro-gram "has also made me a bit more realistic about what I hope to accom-plish. I said just the other day, 'One presidency can't undo generations of mission drift!' So I'm lowering my sights: What can we accomplish on a smaller scale?" He was still looking for voices loyal to the originat-ing vision of the college—but he was less messianic. He had begun to realize that the only vision capable of creating missional coherence in a college lies scattered among its contemporary members, not waiting in the deep past to resume its original ascendancy in the modern college.

Managing Institutional Resistance to Vocational Leadership: Two Cases

The spouse of one of the presidents who came to the program from the trials of an especially difficult presidency wondered at first whether the seminar would do either of them any good. "My initial skepticism," she said, "came from hearing the presidents in particular—and some of the spouses—claim that they had found their 'one true vocation' and that those of us who had our own careers as well as a bunch of different roles in the family and the community had somehow come up short."

But she and several spouses came to realize, while listening to presidents talk about their vocations, "that the presidency was so large a thing in their lives that it actually defined them." This bolt from the blue freed her of embarrassment that she lacked such a singular and consuming vocation. "I began to see that for women like me it was fine *not* to have 'one true vocation.' It kept us more flexible, better able to handle adversity."

She knew of the "conflation error" described in Chapter One from her experience with her husband's current presidency—that those whose fulfillment depends on a particular job are constantly visited by the fear of losing that job or failing in its performance. She and the multi-vocational spouses in her seminar "realized that we didn't fear losing one or another of our roles or vocations because no one of them defined us, as the presidency seemed to define a couple of our spouses."

Her husband had been selected to help the college weather what its trustees understood as a moderate financial crisis. They commissioned the president to straighten out the place by applying more efficient administrative protocols and by raising new capital through philanthropy. Within the first few months of his tenure, however, the new president concluded that the college was in worse shape than he had been told and that it was in need of very deep reform. When he sought to activate the board's promise of collaboration, it rejected his diagnosis and sense of urgency.

"It was a college that had come to see itself as a 'family.' The same firm had audited the books for years. A couple of vendors were represented on the board. There was very little accountability in the college from top to bottom and vice versa; everyone pretty much did his or her own thing. They were autonomous." A comprehensive evaluation of the college's welfare didn't exist and wasn't welcomed.

This clash of diagnoses, with the board taking the view that the college was suffering a common cold and the president seeing the problem as a case of walking pneumonia, exacerbated the traditional tension in academe between the scholar-teacher professionals in the classroom and the "careerists" in administration. Silently supported by a board less worried than the president, elements of the faculty were able to resist the stringent measures sought by the president such as restrictions on positions, program expense, discounted financial aid, and the like.

As this president struggled to find traction against the resistance, he contracted what he agrees is a distinctively vocational illness: Unable to pursue an envisioning process that might have conferred upon him the authority to lead the college, he began to transfer responsibility for its welfare from the college to himself. Weakened by the denial of authority that precipitated this transfer, the problems became worse. As the illness ran its course, the president became increasingly consumed by the massive responsibility that his overweening sense of duty summoned him to accept. By both his own and his spouse's testimony, he was lost to family, friends, and ironically, even his own vocational compass.

Long after he had left the college and had begun to regain his enthusiasm for higher education, he said, "There was a lack of community in that college. I tried to build one by doing what I thought were the best things, in the long run, for the college—regardless of what the impact might be on me." But in the process, he said, "I lost track of the hell I was putting my family through."

Now, well into a "detoxification" interim position, he had come to accept a truth his wife had pointed out early in their participation in the program: "When he allowed the presidency to take the place of his vocation, he lost touch with himself, and so did I." Both of them have since collaborated in drawing up a detailed vocational portrait of him. He described it as follows: "I now realize that my vocation is to make it possible for others to be the very best that they can be; finding the resources, lowering the barriers, but in such a way that they can take the credit . . . to help them from the wings." He went on to say that his had been the "wrong" kind of presidency because of a clash between his leadership style and the college's kind of "followership." "In that college, everyone wanted to be autonomous, to do his or her own thing. I wanted to help 'from the wings'—to get everyone to accept responsibility for what he or she would do for students, for the college. It wasn't that I was trying to impose expectations. I wanted accountability, both for adopting expectations and for meeting them."

He tellingly concluded that he "wanted to lead, although 'from the wings'; they [the college's faculty and staff] were 'followers,' and that's where the real rub came." To the degree that his presidency was true to his vocation, he meant to instill a self-determined purpose and dynamic in the college. This called upon each member to pursue an envisioned version of the college. But as he saw it, the "followers" at that particular college couldn't do that; they were isolated from the community, mired in a restricted range of what they could do guided exclusively by self-interest.

With the strong counsel of his wife, he seems now to see that his super-vocational acceptance of sole responsibility for the welfare of the college was itself a form of "followership." It could not and did not lead toward institutional self-governance or self-determination by means of envisioning. He and the constituents of that college, under those circumstances, were able to create nothing more than an additional chapter in a disoriented saga. They could neither generate nor begin the realization of vocational leadership.

Another president came to the program well into a challenging but modestly successful effort to adapt a college with a carefully maintained religious tradition to the recruiting and placement requirements of a very competitive urban higher education environment. He had come to the presidency of this college out of a natal loyalty to its sponsoring denomination but "was shocked at how little the faculty understood about the 'business' of education."

He took up his presidency as he had taken up his earlier faculty positions—as a teacher—and encountered almost immediately a very complicated resistance from his faculty "students." They came to the defense of the denominational identity of the college against his alleged betrayal of it to the "business" demands of "the market." His credentials as a member of the denomination as well as an experienced member of the professorate were beyond question, and yet he had "been navigating incredibly tough waters" in adapting the college and its denominational tradition to its educational mission. He applied to the program with the enthusiastic support of his spouse so that "we might talk with other presidents and spouses about how to keep up the energy to do this really hard work."

He was surprised to meet presidents at the seminar who had achieved their positions in institutions with which they had no shared heritage. "I had never yet met people who had the unvarnished goal of being a president—and here were several who were in a second presidency and even looking for a third!" "And then," he said, "I noticed that some of the people whose prior experiences were the most disparate from my own were the people that I gravitated to. We seemed to share a common sense of what we were up to in our presidencies." The seminar and informal discussion of institutional mission made this connection clear.

This president pushed a share of the responsibility for the renewal of the college onto the college itself. Hence, he became its counselor in finding a vision that was simultaneously mindful of its denominational tradition and of its obligation to the realities of the world to which it was called to render useful service. The program put him and his spouse in touch with others similarly situated, and he combined this reassuring experience with his knowledge of the college's traditions and the competitive realities of higher education in urban settings to sustain his energy for "this very hard work."

From Mission to the Concept of Saga: Creating Institutional Self-Consciousness

The interest level of the sitting presidents and their spouses leapt noticeably in all three seminars when we reached the third of the four subjects of the inquiry—institutional mission. This was especially true of the presidents themselves, both those who were flourishing and those who came seeking renewal of their energy for the work.

All presidents have a continuing curiosity about the resources of leadership and administration that exist within the institutional structure itself. All seem to agree that a coherent mission fully familiar to every member of the community makes for a good start. But what is the president's role in finding (or creating) and instilling such a mission? And to what extent can a president help create such a mission? And what role does institutional mission play *inside* the college, as distinguished from *outside* the college? A remarkable consensus eventually developed among participating presidents in answer to these questions. This consensus was rooted in our "discovery" that vocational thinking could be as fully applied to the institutional systems of colleges and universities as to their individual presidents.

The subject of institutional mission was introduced in each of the seminars by Burton Clark's assessment in *The Distinctive College* of reforms in the twentieth century at Antioch College, Reed College, and Swarthmore College.[1] According to Clark, these reforms emerged from a dialectic of remarkable presidential leadership, on the one hand, and three different kinds of institutional uncertainty, on the other. The uncertainty at Antioch College was precipitated by a decline in financial resources that threatened survival. At Reed College, it turned up as the college searched for an official statement of its founding purpose and identity. At Swarthmore College, it accompanied an evolving preference for a new institutional self-definition. In each case, the interaction of institutional circumstance and dedicated leadership added a new chapter to the college's "saga," to use Clark's term.

This idea for Clark denotes institutional self-consciousness. It is generated in a college or university by a narrative history that integrates beginnings with consequential events to create a "living" identity. Such an identity combines form and purpose, strategy and tactics. It crystallizes in what he calls the "organizational character" of the college. There, the values of a place become "concretely expressed." Central to organizational character of the preeminently distinctive college, according to Clark, turns out to be "how much [it] believed in itself and in what it was doing."[2]

Having started the inquiry by distinguishing vocation from its distant relatives career and profession, and then bearing down on the conditions, processes, and generic results of vocational discernment, Presidential Vocation and Institutional Mission Program participants quickly were able to see Clark's sagas as a conduit through which

---

1. Burton Clark, "The Making of an Organizational Saga," in *The Distinctive College*, rev. ed. (New Brunswick, N.J.: Transaction Publishers, 1992), 233–262.

2. Ibid., viii–ix.

vocational thinking could be applied to colleges and universities. The implications of this application were exciting to prospective presidents looking for new vocational tasks and especially to those seeking institutional and personal renewal.

As the title of his book indicates, Clark views the three colleges as "distinctive" institutions. He regularly translates "distinctive" as "outstanding," thus bestowing upon these three places the honor claimed by hundreds who describe themselves today as "highly selective." Only one or two of the colleges represented in the Presidential Vocation and Institutional Mission Program endeavor, however, made such a claim. The presidents of these institutions were quite ready to argue that each college and university was "distinctive" but they would not, at least among themselves, claim that their institution was "better" than others. One president, in fact, represented an institution where a trustee made such a comment in the context of receiving a distinguished service award. The trustee referred to Parker Palmer's ideas as expressed in his *Let Your Life Speak* to claim that her college was, in comparison with its peers, "distinctive, but not better."

In any case, the Presidential Vocation and Institutional Mission Program seminars used the concepts of calling and service to the neighbor or community and respect for the careful processes of discernment to build a bridge from Clark's notions of saga in his "outstanding" colleges to vocationism in our "distinctive" colleges. Thus, we transferred to our colleges the same expectation of vocational self-awareness to which we held ourselves. As we discussed this idea, Clark's saga became our "envisioning," which we saw as a deliberative, creative process that yields a yet-to-be-realized college or university. For us, envisioning functioned for institutional mission as discernment functions for personal vocation.

A president and his wife came to the program two years after they discovered that many of their college's constituents thought of the college quite differently from the way it had been described to them during the search process. They came to the program for help in finding a way to reconcile these varying interpretations, and wondered whether they could find it in the history of the college since its founding.

The predominant view among the constituents they met upon arrival was that the college was Christian and evangelical—a far cry from their own insistent secularism and at odds with the portrayal generated by the search committee. Instead of resigning, which felt like (and would probably have been judged as) failure, or trying to impose their secular convictions on the college, they decided "to stick it out." To "honor the school," as they felt obliged to do for contractual, moral, and prudential reasons, they converted their very close marriage into a deliberative redoubt from which they could sally forth to accomplish their administrative work and to which they could retreat for revitalization. In the meantime, they pushed the misalignment itself "under the rug."

Hence, they came to the program determined to confront this mismatch and hoped to "get counsel from others" as to how "we could discharge our responsibilities to the school and its past without undermining or selling out our own beliefs." As they talked this through with their peers in the seminar, they concluded that they were not the ones, as the president put it, "to 'teach' the school a version of its Christianity that would reconcile it to its educational mission." That would feel insincere and would likely look too self-interested to be accepted, even though it may have been intellectually brilliant. The envisioning project, they both thought, "would have to wait for another president."

They were about to turn back, therefore, to the administrative issues that had been preoccupying them—just as the seminar advanced upon the third of its four scheduled subjects: institutional mission. They were so powerfully drawn to the idea of institutional saga and its conversion into vision by the distinctive forms of vocational leadership that they came to the interview, convened about a year later, with a fully developed and half-executed process for finding the core elements of a coherent and compelling self-definition for the college. (This "process" and their reasons for adopting it are detailed in Chapter Three. Suffice it to say here that they found by way of it a partial reconciliation of the fractious voices in the college, but they couldn't find a permanent part for themselves in the new harmony.)

One of the heavy contributors to and beneficiaries of the institutional mission inquiry was a distinguished professor who became president of a college with whose institutional legacy he was profoundly sympathetic. But he came to the program disheartened by institutional resistance to his leadership he hadn't expected. It loosened his attachment to the legacy and immersed him in the daily and tension-ridden business of administering the place. And it seriously threatened his self-confidence. "You know how coaches look for little kids, girls as well as boys, who want the ball, especially when the going gets tough? They want that ball! They believe that they can carry it across the goal line or shoot it in the basket or kick it through the goal. Well, I began to wonder whether I deserved to be given the ball. Am I good enough? These people gave me this trust. Am I really good enough?"

He and his spouse came to the program for relief from the resistance and for the reversal of the self-doubt that it had spawned. The confessional conversation that occurred in his particular seminar revealed that several of his colleagues were suffering a similar malaise. The deliberation about institutional self-definition brought him and several others back to the missions that originally had attracted them to their posts. "The thing that was so wonderful about the program was the healing power of the things we said so openly to each other—and which we remember and repeat when we see each other at conferences and meetings now. Those conversations brought us back to the 'saga' of our place. It reinspired us to continue to do the work—because, man, I sure couldn't do it for those characters that were fighting with me there every day!"

This thrill of "reinspiration" became palpable among us in varying degrees in all three of the seminars for presidents. As the interviews confirmed, it has continued to inspire remarkable thinking and work. Perhaps we had stumbled upon a whole new form of the American college and university presidency in which a vitalizing collaboration of president and institution takes the place of the exhausting separation of leader and led.

From Saga to Vision: The Vocational President as Student of the College

Ironically, the expansion of the president's vocational duty from the presidency per se to the clarification and integrity of the college's mission relieved the burden of personal responsibility being borne by presidents whose work was meeting resistance on campus. The conversion of Clark's sagas into institutional vocations and of his visionaries into more sophisticated envisioners put presidents into a new kind of relationship with their campuses.

A dean who had caught himself just short of accepting the presidency of a college that "wanted him" came to the program as the two-year president of an institution that "needed him." For him and for his spouse, the seminar inquiry on institutional mission was the high point of the program. "I came to this university out of what I felt was mutual need—me of it and it of me. When I accepted the presidency, I thought I knew what strategic initiatives to pursue for the sake of the college's welfare. What I didn't understand correctly were ways to launch those initiatives or to rationalize their congruence with the particular culture, welfare, and language of the institution." The missing knowledge, he said, "began to come to me as I listened to alumni, faculty, and staff discuss and question my leadership. And I learned how to speak for the institution and how to reflect the institution in what I said."

The university, he discovered, was a "who" rather than a "what," and like the discerning vocationist, it must "know itself." It was this president's active listening, the fruits of which he summed up from time to time by his refined practice of forensic rhetoric, that eventually supplied the university with a coherent and compelling self-definition. And he knew, as vocational presidents in particular eventually do, that forensic rhetoric is both the form and substance of institutional and personal self-definition.

A principal result of starting our discussion of institutional mission with Clark's sagas, and making our way from there to envisioning, was to dethrone "strategy" and "strategic planning" from their high seats among the arts of institutional revitalization. Clark had hinted that his sagas were the parents of the strategic plans that the three colleges devised to extract themselves from crisis, not the siblings and certainly not the children. But his saga-making presidents struck several members of each seminar as "visionary" rather than "vocational." To them, Clark's presidents seemed *charismatic* in Max Weber's sense. The presidents participating in the Presidential Vocation and Institutional Mission Program were far too modest to accept any such account of their own leadership.

One of the presidents who had just been selected by a financially troubled college found inspiration in the institutional mission discussion to plan the envisioning process he would initiate as soon as he got back to campus. His board pulled him off this envisioning work within months of beginning it when it didn't immediately reverse the slide in financial indicators. They wanted a strategic plan instead. He did not protest. He simply gathered his cabinet and generated a program-development, recruiting, and expense reduction plan in record time and turned immediately back to envisioning in order to inspire the community to embrace and activate the plan. "I knew that a plan without a vision would fail, but the board thought otherwise." About a year after he returned to envisioning, the plan started to gain traction. "Even the board began to see that *this* initiative belonged in the plan and *that* one didn't."

Another president, who had been wrestling with his board over the definition of the college for which both were to be held liable, said in the interview that while a personal life can be purposely constructed if one's calling is accurately discerned, a college or university can't be so constructed or reconstructed by even the most vocationally oriented president. "It is not about my coming to make the college look more like me. Nor is it about the trustees remaking the college according to a corporate image or into the shape it had when they were students there." Instead, he said, "A vocational president tries to tease out of the college its own highest potential."

In a convocation speech inaugurating the envisioning process to which he and the trustees eventually agreed, he argued against taking any peer, including highly regarded ones, as a model for either the college's self-definition or its eventual strategic plan. At the risk of seeming imperious, he also rejected consideration of even surefire, new-net-revenue initiatives unless they appeared consistent with the core identity of the college. "We're going to be the best 'us' that we can be," he said. "So we had better start with some very basic, very local questions: Who are we? Where did we come from? Where are we now?"

He referred to Jim Collins' popular book *Good to Great* to draw a clear line between vocational presidents and leaders who bring their own visions to the presidency.[3] Collins, he said, "had taken a firm stand against 'visionary' leaders. His most successful CEOs delayed pronouncing the vision until they had an internally validated basis for it."

---

3. Jim Collins, *Good to Great: Why Some Companies Make the Leap . . . and Others Don't* (New York: Harper Business, 2001).

The modesty of vocational presidents and of Collins' "Level 5 Leaders," as he described "great" CEOs, caused both to look to the collective wisdom of the college or corporation for guidance in capitalizing on institutional crises, or even moments of communal uncertainty, to sharpen institutional self-definition. Both vocational presidents and "great" CEOs seem acutely aware that strategic plans not squared with institutional culture lack durability as well as immediate effectiveness.

The Dialectic of Envisioning

The interviews turned up several stories describing the dialectic that operates between a vocational president and an envisioning institution. All of them suggest that the interaction brings new self-knowledge to president and institution alike. One story that made that point especially well was of a dean who had successfully led his faculty through a general education revision, guided by the idea of vocation. He later moved on to the presidency of a college that in very literal terms needed an envisioning process.

The college that appointed him to the presidency had lost momentum and missional definition by high turnover on the board, in several other executive positions, and in the presidency. Although it was founded by a church body, its denominational identity had weakened. The new president was not familiar enough with the college's history to know what founding principles or traditions might be embraced by the modern constituents. The president had been a student of the educational philosophy of the sponsoring denomination of the college, but wasn't at all sure how to "package" this knowledge to legitimize acceptance by his contemporaries.

The discussion in his seminar for prospective presidents convinced him that the visions that obtain traction in colleges and universities are, above all, realistic. If the vision is so dream-like that it lacks relevance to the institution's policies, processes, and daily life, it never can be made part of the ethos of the place. A vision that imbibes elements of the institution's "must do" agenda gives those elements new legitimacy and by the same interactive process adds authority to the vision.

But the president had also learned from his experience that a vision without an image of the college as it might become would inevitably bog down in the operational realities of the present. The proposition that institutional vision takes form in the effort to articulate it is closely allied with the argument that the vision emerges from the homogenization of the institution's past, present, and future.

To begin the process, the new president convinced the board chair to convene an agenda-less retreat at which the trustees would be asked to "talk about the future of the college." At the president's suggestion, the chair assembled the trustees with the request that they "discuss the future without feeling compelled to reach a conclusion about what to do about it and when." Although the retreat generated the outline of a portrait of the envisioned college, which the president then tested with other constituents, it did not produce an agenda of tasks to complete. Both the president and the chair responded vigorously to the predictable complaint of the administrators among the trustees that "we just spent a day and we don't have anything to show for it."

The president purveyed the fledgling vision in each of his appearances in the community, to the Rotary, the Lions Club, the Chamber of Commerce, the alumni board, and class gatherings. At first, he accepted invitations to speak only if a reception preceded his presentation. That way he could be sure to tailor his remarks after the lunch or dinner and in some measure respond to the informal conversations that took place earlier over the canapés. Hence, he was learning about his institution's vision as he was taught it: he was assembling it from (and reacting to it in) the perspectives to which he listened.

Both his and his spouse's interest in the presidency rose dramatically when they realized in their prospectives seminar that equivalents of

Clark's sagas in less distinctive colleges could be converted into "visions" by applying the reflective practices of vocational discernment to institutional history. So far, his envisioning work, which he understands as a special kind of "historiography," has typecast his presidency as a "listening" and "attentive" one. He credits this fact with giving his leadership a legitimacy that has allowed him to weaken and redirect the centrifugal forces that had gathered momentum on the campus from the turnover of leadership.

He uses rhetoric artfully from every lectern he is given and intends to infuse the processes of envisioning into the culture of the college. And he is insisting that members of his inner circle pay similar attention to their own speeches and policies. The nature of the vision that finally emerges from the effort, he is consistent in stating, will depend upon what new institutional self-knowledge comes from the effort in the meantime. He knows that his own capacity to recognize "new knowledge" will depend upon refining his own vocational discernment.

Several presidents, including some from among the facilitators, have remarked on the operation of this dialectic, but none see it as troubling. One of the presidents who participated in the program came to see vocational life as giving shape to the vocationist as the vocationist gives shape to the college. "You may enter a presidency for career reasons," he said in the interview, "but if you stick with it, it likely will become a vocation. You just can't stay twelve years or even eight and say, 'I just did this for a job.'" A president without a "bigger picture" of the envisioned college in mind, he said, "couldn't actually 'do' a presidency, just as one couldn't be an economist, accountant, academic theorist, strategic planner, or fund-raiser, without understanding and acknowledging how it all ties together. And you can't make other people, such as trustees, faculty, your own executive team, better friends of the college unless you can show this group the 'bigger picture.'" He concluded with the aid of a metaphor: "It's 'mission' that forms the parameters of our existence.

That's the frame that contains the picture of our institution. And we as presidents are inside the frame, changing shape as we change the shape of the college."

In fact, vocational presidents who have been unable for one reason or another to mount effective envisioning processes have felt the consequences in certain peculiar weaknesses in their administration of the college. A president was hired as a compatriot by a board that was proud of the college that the trustees, themselves, thought *they* had been running during a lengthy interim. They wanted the faculty, staff, and students enthusiastically to embrace their contented view and hired the new president with that purpose in mind. Unexpectedly, the new president showed interest in accomplishing changes that would strengthen the institution, including reforms like widening accessibility in both enrollment and placement, and thereby upgrading the capacity of the college to educate. Certain trustees interpreted these reforms as criticisms of the board's oversight.

The trustees had expected to convince the president of their contented view by welcoming the president into their cultural milieu. But that milieu didn't suit the taste of the new president. The president's unwillingness to join was not motivated by policy or governance issues or even by disagreement with the board's view of the institution. Nevertheless, the resulting tension foreshadowed problems in that presidency in two respects. It prevented the institution from revealing itself more fully to the board through an envisioning process facilitated by the president, and it denied the president the authority to execute prudent or necessary improvements.

One of the symptoms of this circumstance was that when the president eventually resigned, the members of the college cabinet felt abandoned. In the absence of an envisioning process that might have supplied the preliminary form of an institutional self-definition, the president had become the focal point of his colleagues' loyalty. Among other things, this challenged the president's humility. It amounted to a clinging dependence that turned vice presidents into personal charges rather than fellow citizens of the emergent college civitas. Such dependence exhausted the president of the energy otherwise available to the once and future college and it prevented cultivation of the civility that helps to produce that civitas. Moreover, it denied those within the institution the security of a record that reflected solid collaboration in the achievement of institutional improvement.

The Forensic Rhetoric of the Vocational Presidency

The vocational president's derivation of political authority from the envisioning process makes of the president ipso facto the very voice of the college. The core of the president's muse is vision. The "power" of such presidencies is entirely lodged, therefore, in rhetoric. Brief consideration in the seminars of two of Abraham Lincoln's speeches, the "Second Inaugural" and his "Speech to the Young Men's Lyceum at Springfield" (1838), enabled the group to notice this fact.

Seminar participants encountered Lincoln as they explored the transformation of Clark's sagas into envisioning and the emergent image of the once and future college. We read Lincoln's speech of 1838 as his conscious embrace of America's founding at Philadelphia and his rejection of the greater personal glory in the rising chaos of mid-century malaise over slavery. He appeared, therefore, as a vocationist rather than as a visionary, and his rhetoric functioned as both instrument and registry of a reenvisioned America. Lincoln chose from his own proclivities and from something he called "political religion" to summarize the vision and make it inspiring:

> As the patriots of seventy-six did to the support of the Declaration
> of Independence, so to the support of the Constitution and laws,
> let every American . . . remember that to violate the law, is to

trample on the blood of his father, and to tear the charter of his own, and his children's liberty. Let reverence for the laws be breathed by every American mother, to the lisping babe, that prattles on her lap; let it be taught in schools, in seminaries, and in colleges; let it be written in primers, spelling books, and in almanacs; let it be preached from the pulpit, proclaimed in legislative halls, and enforced in the courts of justice. And, in short, let it become the *political* religion of the nation. . . .[4]

The group heard Lincoln's soaring rhetoric and joined for just a moment his young audience at Springfield. They sensed, as the members of the lyceum must have done, the emergence of the new "political religion." To emphasize the formative role of rhetoric in the vocational president's arsenal for converting constituents into citizens, the group took notice of Lincoln's consistent effort from 1838 to his Second Inaugural to adapt the America founded at Philadelphia to the mid-nineteenth century civil crisis and Reconstruction.

Seminar participants used the "Second Inaugural" speech to suggest a critical aspect of the kind of rhetoric the envisioning president might well use to acknowledge the political victories that necessarily mark the emergence of the vocational college. No gloating is apparent in this address. Lincoln presented the war as inevitable. He blamed it on fate and credited the victory neither to North nor South but instead to the nation and to the great experiment in freedom launched by the Revolution. The war had perpetuated that experiment but at a terrible price. It was now time to do that which only communities, remembering their humanity, can do: "to bind up the nation's wounds; to care for him who shall have borne the battle, and for his widow, and his orphan—to do all which may achieve and cherish a just, and a lasting peace, among

---

4. Abraham Lincoln, *Selected Speeches and Writings* (New York: Library of America/Vintage Books, 1992), 449–450.

ourselves, and with all nations."[5] We thought that famous paragraph contained good counsel to the vocational presidents successfully leading a college through the minefield of disagreements among constituents toward the realization of its vision. We all realized that, though Lincoln's rhetoric is the gold standard for raising a vision out of a saga, its biblical references and patriotism must be moderated to move the constituencies of modern academe toward institutional citizenship.

Vocational Humility and the Self-Confidence of Envisioning

The excitement from institutional leaders that welled up in each seminar from the discovery that institutional saga could become institutional vocation by means of envisioning was grounded in the discovery that we could now explore the concepts of calling, service, responsibility, and discernment as they applied to two subjects: ourselves and our colleges.

When the vocational discernment of the college becomes the primary responsibility of the vocational president, the vocational leader ad hominem moves onto a higher plane of self-confidence. As vocational presidents, these humble men and women could now apply the distinctive instruments of vocational leadership—envisioning, an artful use of rhetoric, the projection of the "once and future" community as polity—free of the restraint of self-censure. As this reality dawned upon the presidents participating in the program, a relieved and voluble collegiality broke out among them.

The self-confidence resulting from the direct applicability of vocational discernment to college practices displaced the notable self-doubt confessed by the sitting presidents in all three seminars. "Every solid, good, decent human being I know," said one the presidents participating in the vocation-mission program, "has a tender self. 'Am I good enough to do this,' they ask. 'Do I know enough?' And the great thing about

---

5. Ibid., 283.

the conversation in the seminar over how we lead our colleges with this heavy baggage of self-doubt is that the conversation, itself, cleared the problem. At least it did for me." This president's spouse said that by the time the inquiry reached the discussion of saga, vision, and the importance of speech-making, "we were long past the point when people worried about whether, if they revealed this or that, they would have become less than other people in the seminar." Both this president and his spouse credited the confessional aspects of this seminar for his new enthusiasm for leadership.

The complementary intersection between presidential vocationism and the humility of vocationists is revealed in a dozen vignettes that were collected during the interviews. They illustrate that vocational presidents widened the sway of the emergent vision by distributing credit for their own achievements among their vice presidents, deans, trustees, spouses, and colleagues. Sharing vignettes that demonstrated that magnanimous distribution of credit is far more fulfilling than the taking of it led us to see that what most attracts the vocationist is the close association with others in a cause rather than the mantle of the founder. As in the case of the president in Chapter One, who allowed credit for his fund-raising acumen to go to others, the resulting "association" is not only with one's immediate associates but with those who founded the tradition that the envisioning is reinterpreting or even refounding. That president knew that the college's collaboratively constructed self-definition and vision required his own retreat. Unless he took himself out of the way, the emerging college would lack room to keep on growing.

The Vocational Presidency as "Level 5" Leadership

This dialectic between the persona of the president and the institution-defining myths of the vision illustrates what Jim Collins has noted as a critical trait of "Level 5" leadership. In *Good to Great*, which may have been more carefully and widely read in American academe than in the corporate world and holds something of a biblical position among both presidents and prospective presidents who participated in the program, Collins reports that the leaders whose companies outperformed their peers over a twenty-year period were "modest." They took the blame for things that went wrong, and handed out praise to others for things that went right.[6]

The interviews of presidents in the Presidential Vocation and Institutional Mission Program suggest that this is a common trait among vocationists, whether they seek to legitimize a corporation's or a college's vision. The dollop of authority that makes the dough of vision rise, so to speak, into a full-fledged loaf comes from the president and is transferred slowly during the envisioning process to the vision itself. In the best leaders, this process is intended to be continuing.

Collins had chosen the Lincoln we met in the 1838 speech to exemplify another Level 5 leadership trait that is consistent with institutional envisioning: Lincoln as well as the corporate CEOs Collins identified as "great" were committed above all to succession, not of themselves but of their envisioned institutions.[7]

In a thirty-five-page supplement to *Good to Great*, in which Collins applies the formula for greatness to nonprofits, he makes clear that this commitment to succession qualifies for Level 5 leadership designation only if the commitment is neither to a CEO him or herself nor to the mere survival of the corporate entity. Instead, it must be to the culture and business strategy that made the company "great." We took these attributes as equivalents of our institutional "visions" and the strategic plans by which vocational presidents seek to bring them to life.

6. Jim Collins, *Good to Great and the Social Sectors: A Monograph to Accompany "Good to Great"* (New York: HarperCollins, 2005), 22–23.

7. Ibid.

The model of Level 5 leadership Collins explicates in his work struck us as ready-made for vocationists in all segments of modern society. Far from being exclusively applicable in the corporate world—indeed, the subtitle of his supplement on nonprofits is *Why Business Thinking Is Not the Answer*—Collins makes clear that Level 5 leadership is distinctively political rather than economic or administrative and may be especially useful to vocational presidents in American academe. This discovery was particularly welcome because we had concluded that nothing is quite so civic as vocation, not because it is carried out in public life but because it is dedicated to public life.

Conclusion

Several challenges are unique to vocational presidents: the challenge to develop the kind of deeply relational authority that can facilitate envisioning in place of the more rank-based authority often thought to mark efficient administration; the challenge to establish a credible scholastic understanding of the college's history and traditions as anchors of one's artful use of rhetoric in behalf of its vision; the challenge to reconcile the idealism of vocationism with a realistic diagnosis of human and institutional possibilities in this world and at this moment; and the challenge to resist the fusion of one's vocation with that of the institution (a powerful temptation that rises in the all-absorbing effort to "do one's duty"). Of all these challenges, however, none may be as difficult as finding a sustaining energy for the work.

Even though a huge reservoir of this sustaining energy is available in the exhilarating liberation from the restraints of modesty that vocation so wonderfully enables, it cannot possibly be enough to bear the burden of the presidency. Something more is needed—something personal but not private—which reconciles personal integrity with the other-directedness that is required of community development and community service.

CHAPTER 3

Inspiring and Sustaining the Vocational Presidency

At least seventy of America's independent colleges and universities have been or are now being led by "graduates" of the Presidential Vocation and Institutional Mission Program. All thirty of the program's alumni interviewed for this book reported that their participation in its seminars changed their approach to the presidency and raised the level of their personal satisfaction in the work.

In this chapter, we will explore the testimony of those participants whose commitment to the presidency was restored or embellished by the experience. What factors had made them question their suitability for the presidency in the first place? What about the program and, in particular, about the idea of vocation do they credit for their renewed enthusiasm and energy for the work? What, exactly, were the sources of this enthusiasm, and how sustainable are those sources proving to be?

The Centrality of "Cause" in Vocational Life: The First Case

One of the presidents who credited the program with putting him in close touch with himself "for the first time in years" observed that "a presidency has a way of supplying you with both direction and energy.

When you're up to your neck in the job, you don't have to worry about running out of gas. You're just swept along by the pace and endless duties of the position." But the president who allows this and who relies on the pounding rhythms of the work for both direction and energy must eventually suspect, he thought, that his or her life is "out of control."

Vocation, he said, demands a more intense and differently focused attentiveness than does a career fired by ambition. As a vocationist, "you're trying to line up your life with your self—not with who your friends think you are or who you think your friends think you are." The "self-awareness" this requires involves a combination of "who you are" and "who you would like to be." Both he and his spouse credited the extraordinary candor of the conversations inspired by the program's mixture of readings, peers, spouses, and facilitators for bringing him back to himself.

He reports that he and his spouse made good use of these insights during the final years of his presidency, especially to bear the incipient criticisms of constituencies and to reduce his remaining cache of self-doubt. But the most valuable payoff of these insights occurred in retirement. As he prepared to resume the scholarship and teaching that he laid aside for the presidency, he found himself "flitting" from task to task, hoping to recreate a sense of usefulness that both he and his spouse associated with the pure busyness of the presidency.

It turned out that it wasn't the busyness of the presidency that he missed; it was the sense of being useful to someone other than himself, including his immediate family. As he prepared syllabi for his teaching responsibilities and prospectuses for the several research projects he was considering, he wondered how or whether his courses and scholarship might benefit from his own recent consideration of vocation and mission. This led him to a sudden and surprising realization: neither he nor his professional colleagues had "paid sufficient attention to self-awareness," either of the progenitors of their field of study, of themselves, or of the students of the subject. That realization stopped the "flitting," according to his spouse, and settled him down to the difficult but enthralling task of fixing this deficiency and fitting it into his work.

"Until you know who you are," said his spouse in explaining the excitement they shared in the new purpose of his scholarship, "you can't expect a successful outcome from your leadership. Or you may have a successful outcome but you'll lose a lot of sleep worrying about things catching up with you—wondering when others might find out things about you that you don't want them to know."

The excitement they both see in his "repair" of the professional scholarship in his field of study has sharpened and deepened his sense of calling. He now means to enlarge and enrich the public sphere of life in his profession, family, and community by finding and describing the reciprocal relationship between self-awareness and community service. He continues to think of the "wonderful connectivity" that transformed relative strangers in their vocation-mission seminar into friends and counselors, and of the clearer discernment that catalyzed his attempt to reform his own professional field.

As the two of them recounted the revitalizing effect of this new project, the president added an important further comment. He said that this change in perspective regarding his discipline would never have occurred to him before his presidency. "I came from a deanship in my field of study to my presidency," he remembered, "on account of ambition. And the ambition was activated purely by opportunity. I was offered two presidencies within a week of each other, and thought, 'Okay! Let's do it.' I didn't really think about whether I had the makings of a president—and certainly didn't wonder whether I was called to it. What mattered was that several people in two different universities thought I was qualified to do it." But the presidency led him to the Presidential Vocation and Institutional Mission Program which, in turn, prompted him to think anew about the causes and satisfactions of his engagement in academic life.

The Centrality of "Cause" in Vocational Life: The Second Case

Another president came to the interview just after launching a promising initiative to find among the members of his cabinet and faculty the makings of a coherent collegiate self-image from which an animating vision for the college might be formed. The president and his spouse had been surprised to learn when they first arrived that the college did not, in fact, think of itself as they had been led to believe both by the board and by their own experience in the search. In fact, they found it impossible to narrow the number of identities its constituents proposed for the college to a group of two or three that were close enough to each other to offer a possibility of concatenation. Every constituency seemed to them to be at odds with every other.

This lack of a cohering institutional self-definition was the cause, in the president's view, of the "major disarray" that he soon discovered in the administrative organization, procedures, and policies of the college. Straightening out the administration became his first order of business. Given the lack of a common institutional self-image, the president and his spouse bore the brunt of the effort on the narrow span of their personal authority as "the new president and his wife." The effort, of course, was greeted neither with universal acclaim nor universal criticism. Hence, the initial passage of the presidency was rocky for all.

But the three or four years it took them to straighten out the operational life of the college yielded the couple new standing and authority. At that point in time, they came to the program. They specifically sought to learn how they might leverage their success in order to bring cohesion to the self-definitional incoherence of the institution.

The president explained that his success in getting control of operations did not reach deeply enough into the core identity of the college to pull it together or to end the misalignment he and his spouse felt just after his selection. "I had hoped that, over a period of time, the college would adapt to us and we to them. I knew that these institutions are terrifically resilient, but I didn't see—as I do now—that this is because they are relatively insensitive to change, whether it be cultural, economic, or political."

So they came to the program looking for ways to extend the reach of their leadership on behalf of institutional coherence. They were drawn in by the formal and informal discussion of saga and its conversion into vision. They returned to campus with several winning ideas for launching an envisioning effort that they supposed would complement the administrative reforms with new strategic initiatives in the college's marketing, pedagogical, and governance procedures.

At the same time, however, the president and his spouse had come to believe that the college's vision could never include them and that their misalignment with the college would remain after any authentic institutional self-definition resulted from their envisioning work. Finding and articulating a comprehensive saga for the college was their presidential duty, but the distance between their personal convictions and the college's history and circumstance—the ground for any institutional vision—was too great ever to be bridged. The Presidential Vocation and Institutional Mission Program clearly contributed to extending their tenure in that presidency while merely postponing the date of their resignation.

As soon as they got back from the summer meetings of their seminar, they began to solicit constituents, beginning with the faculty, for alternative views of the college's mission, and hit pay dirt right off the bat. Several faculty, proud of the college's record of "taking average kids and making them terrific," as the president put it in the interview, revealed in a regimen of conversations around the presidential dinner table that they, themselves, had benefited from just such a transformative experience. Others confessed that their particular interest in teaching students, some of whom had been injured by abuse, was rooted in their own experience and survival of mistreatment. Yet others sensed nascent bonds that might cross departmental and divisional boundaries through the sharing of these pedagogical sympathies. They contributed news of their own discoveries of exceptional figures among the "average" students at their colleges who similarly had been transformed.

The general result has been a shift in the faculty mood from regret, disappointment, and a divisive competitiveness to a celebration of the college as a safe haven from poverty of opportunity and other inequities, a haven well furnished with therapies of enlightenment and self-understanding propounded by faculty colleagues who had, by fortuitous circumstance, wound up where they were most needed.

The president and his spouse thus facilitated the birth of a campus civitas. It was borne of a new familiarity among long-standing colleagues who publicly answered before each other two basic questions: "Why is each of us here? What keeps us, one by one, at this work?" The discussion did not devolve into interdisciplinary repartee or exchanges concerning the comparative contributions of departments to institutional reputation; it transcended that plane. Indeed, the first stirring of policy that emerged from this development was to reenvision what general education regimen might best serve the reawakened college—an area of potential reform that they would not have considered even approaching a year earlier.

When they came to the interview, the president and his spouse had only begun to exploit this widening pool of familiarity in search of an institutional vision. The promise they detected in these fledgling results restored a good part of the self-confidence they had lost when they realized the college that had chosen them had not portrayed itself accurately.

They confessed that they had handled this glaring fact by turning away from the misalignment to the pressing work of operational repair, comforting themselves with what turned out to be false hopes—that "the institution would slowly adapt" to administrative rationality and that it would discover itself in the clarity of its own operational efficiency. Had that occurred, it may not have solved the problem of misalignment, but mutual acknowledgement among the "departmentalized" departments of the college that each needed the other to advance their separate interests might have masked it.

The spouse then came upon an idea that she found especially promising—just as the public discussions among constituents was beginning around her dinner table. "Our conversation about the college's vocation started us thinking about our own. We noticed that the college and each of us had from time to time been derailed from our respective sagas. We could see this in the college because we could see it in our autobiographies. One response to all this," she said, "is to acknowledge the particular derailments" and find in that exercise "a knowledge of what the vocational path should have been. But then, we thought, maybe the derailments form the saga, *are* the saga!"

After observing that such a view makes "what happens" into "what was supposed to happen," she observed that this compounds a delusion to which vocationists are particularly prone.

> You can fool yourself and you can fool others that you're still on your path when you're not. Part of the purpose of our having these public discussions is to pull us all back from the local news occurrences of the moment to a wider time horizon. The "project development" language of envisioning can create the illusion that some particular event or occurrence is essential. But, if you look deeper, you see that it's direction that's the key. That's the track!

She clearly meant that on a route oriented by overarching purpose, far fewer derailments occur than on an itinerary made ad hoc and adjusted daily.

The president then asked a question that resumed the discussion of envisioning, which he saw as the next stage of his presidency: "Do you think that one can be an effective president if he or she is also a beloved part of the community?" He didn't mean "celebrated" or even "admired." "I'm talking," he said, "about a deeper personal love, the kind that sustains people individually and allows them to sit down with associates or acquaintances and talk freely."

"Talking freely" is what he and his wife had been doing for years and what they had done and admired in others during the seminar. And it was what he wanted more of in the college to move his presidency forward. "I'm still thinking that there is a core part of human identity that always seeks really deep personal friendship," he said. "That's hard to achieve for yourself as the president of a small college. But it may be something that the president can somehow give to the college, even though the college cannot give it to the president. That, to me, would be a fulfilling achievement."

He had come to see the rocky period of his presidency as a necessary orientation of the college to him and of him and his wife to the college. He said that during the twenty-year tenure of his predecessor, "Most members of the college had developed strategies to get around or fly under the president's radar. The faculty and staff were so habituated to these strategies that they didn't, and actually couldn't, notice" that the new president differed from the previous one both in style and purpose. "When I would make what I thought were sensitive, fair and prudent decisions, I was surreptitiously criticized as 'aristocratic,' just as my predecessor had been."

But the rocky period of his presidency—and his success in mastering the college's administrative operations—had eventually clarified and confirmed the distinctive style and identity of his role. What was now needed was a process that would clarify and confirm the distinctive identity of the college that would clearly include, from the president's personal vision, talking freely as a hallmark of the envisioned culture.

Sustaining the Vocational "Cause": The Third Case

These two presidents, radically different in age, training, and experience, were anxious to go beyond running the college in one case, or resuming a conventional scholastic career in the other. They each wanted to do more, and hence they struck out in search of a community in which the proclivities of the individual would be reconciled with and guided by that community, or, in particular, a "once and future" version of it. If either one had meant the opposite—that the proclivities of iconoclastic individuals alone should guide the formation of a self-governing and life-giving community—he or she would have been far less interested in accepting the responsibilities of leadership. They embraced those responsibilities so that they might do for others what others had done for them—to reveal the fruits (energy, creativity, hope) that came, in the one case, from high self-awareness in the midst of a "wonderful connectivity" among relative strangers, and, in the other, from "talking freely," which, if properly led, would transform colleagues into friends.

The collegiate community preferred by a third president depended heavily upon friendship, but of a different kind than has so far been explored here. For this president, friendship served to protect his ideal of community rather than to discover or create it. It turns out that his friends, whom he is "very fortunate" to know, do not know each other. Instead, the president himself is the center from which lines run to each friend and back. Only he could call for collective action, and it's not clear whether any would occur if he did. There is no "together," no network, among them.

He shares with his friends, he says, "an inordinate humor that is deeply rooted in the absurd. We point out and deride the profound ridiculousness of much of our modern culture. That has been essential to my stubborn pursuit of teaching and learning—and, I think, to theirs." The humor acknowledges and thereby seeks to weaken the "absurd" closed-mindedness in the very heart of the academy: professors and "experts" who know rather than wonder, who announce rather than ask. For the president, other absurdities that imperil education and blunt its transformative and sanguinary effects include the relentless assault of information technology on literacy—text messaging, self-isolating and conversation-stopping habits of the "plugged-in" generation, the substitution of information for thought as the distinguishing mark of intelligence—and the overwhelming ignorance of the past on the part of those who enroll in his college and too often on the part of those who teach them.

While he appreciates Aristotle's description of friendship as the love of the good that is found in the friend, he finds the calculus cold. "Without a love for one's friends per se that transcends the rational or explicable, there can't be the joy that comes from naming, and thereby dismissing, the absurd and absolutely crazy things that people do every day." This president uses friendship to confirm the propriety and profound fragility of the "great work" to which he has given his life. Holding fast to unadulterated "professional" standards of education is his clear duty and the fixed guide of his presidency. While he does whatever he can through rhetoric and policy to promote the people and parts of his college that share this passion, he feels no need to convert its saga into a vision. He is alone with his God in the cultivation of self-discipline and the college's dedication to the needs of the communities it serves, and he relies upon his friends to sustain him in the project and to keep him at the work.

In respect to his discernment of the calling that undergirds his life and his presidency, he used the Presidential Vocation and Institutional Mission Program as he does his friends. "Just seeing those words, 'vocation' and 'mission,' in the title of the program reminded me," he said, "of how wearing our responsibilities are and how the many pressures of the job push us away from the core work. I came [to the program] to escape those pressures and to think seriously about the fundamental truths that I decided at an early age should inform my personal life as well as my public work with colleagues. I wanted to double check my own loyalty to those ideas, and to review how I was applying them in the presidency."

How well did the program serve him as a college president? "My shyness," he answered, "causes me great anxiety in anticipation of such a self-exposing experience. But it always turns out to be a great and reassuring pleasure to be with colleagues when someone says something truly arresting, something that expresses particularly well something that you believe is true for you, and you all agree, out of your collegiality, that the statement is significant." He extended the description of such "reassuring pleasures" into his own distinctive intellectual aerie: "Sometimes the arresting remark surprises you as well as the colleagues. You think, 'How could anybody doing what I do as a college president say that they simply love their work, for example, and are perfectly at peace with themselves in the doing of it?'"

This president was leading an urban college that had struggled mightily to provide accessibility and a genuine liberal arts education to first-generation students. But he had come to the program to test the perceptiveness of his belief that "vocation, or the attempt to live out a vocation, is why I entered the world of education in the first place." He didn't need friendship for this test; he needed the collegiality of peers to whom he could quietly test the discernment of his calling and the compatibility of his life and work with his sense of vocation. That some of these peers were thinking about their own and their college's mission in secular terms was a boon to him. "Because my understanding of vocation is tied to faith, I accomplished my purpose in coming to the seminar when I came up against understandings of vocation that are so differently rooted in the soul. It brought back to the forefront of my attention the things that I knew were most important to me, but from which the frenetic pace of the presidency had separated me—at least temporarily."

The self to which the program meetings restored this president had been formed and finished in the distant days of youth. It was secured on a daily basis against the corrosive forces of popular culture, as he perceived them, by the nature of his friendships. The program itself functioned for him as a retreat in the classic sense—a personal homecoming accomplished by his remarkable attentiveness and quiet but intense responsiveness to the confessional remarks of his fellow retreaters. And thus he returned to his presidency, restored and refocused.

The Centrality of "Cause" in Vocational Life: The Fourth Case

Yet another president, a declared atheist, had led his college through a veritable resurrection and came to the program wondering what had motivated him, in the absence of a call, to give his life in the first place to higher education, and in the second place to stick with it despite the unremitting challenges and pressures of the work.

During the interview, his studied answer to the second question (about sustaining vocational commitment) was "integrity." For him, integrity is necessarily a "this worldly" concept, but he defined it to include corrective and reforming elements that most of his colleagues normally located in an alternate world.

Moreover, integrity plays a role in his ideal of an awakened college comparable to the role it plays for an awakened president. "I might have used some other word to identify what I mean by integrity, but I'm comfortable with it in part because it transfers so easily from personal to institutional life. For me, it means always operating from the highest degree of honesty possible; in the college, it encourages truth telling and, to the degree that truth telling is regularly accomplished, the result is trustworthiness."

For this president, personal integrity connects closely with institutional integrity. In both cases, the issue is "seeking and telling the truth." If both president and institution have integrity, the one is granted authority to speak for the college, and the other makes the rhetoric believable. As a result, for example, fund-raising by a trustworthy president on behalf of a trusted institution will be impressively successful, as he claimed it had been in the case of his own institution.

Can vocational life—lived by those who render service to this world with principles derived from another—be somehow replicated by presidents who are intent upon reforming their colleges but reject any two-worlds or two-kingdoms perspective? The answer from this president is a resounding yes. For him, the two different worlds are the "determinedly honest man," on the one hand, and popular opinion, on the other. He regularly quotes Lillian Hellman's response to the House Un-American Activities Committee subpoena of her in 1952 to identify "communists and traitors." She said, "I cannot and will not cut my conscience to fit this year's fashions."[1]

Dedication to integrity on the part of himself and his college made of this president the college's most knowledgeable historian. He dug into the traditions of the college to find among its founders and progenitors the seeds of a mission especially fit for modern circumstance. Finding it allowed him to weave into a single story a rhetorically reconstructed version of the school's natal identity with his own long-standing fascination with and professional competence in "assessing the current realities of higher education." "Telling this story in its fullness," as he puts it, has among other things attracted significant philanthropy from alumni and neighbors who have recognized themselves and their forebears in the narrative. This "recognizability" of the envisioned college in the

---

1. Lillian Hellman, to the Committee on Un-American Activities of the U.S. House of Representatives, May 19, 1952.

community is, for this president, evidence that his own trustworthiness has been successfully transferred to the institution.

It also has contributed to the president's sustained interest in the presidency. The experience of having twice facilitated the development of a college that "walks the talk" of the vision his leadership has supplied has both depended upon and contributed to his profound self-confidence. Ultimately, however, the source of his self-confidence is his own integrity rather than his service to a cause rooted in another world.

One of the proofs he offered of his successful transfer of personal integrity into the college was an interchange with an employee at a staff appreciation luncheon about the time he came to the Presidential Vocation and Institutional Mission Program. The employee had asked him during his on-campus interviews for the presidency several years earlier, "What is the name of the person who's been emptying your trash?" She said the president had quickly answered, "Jose." The president asked the employee why she was struck by this exchange and heard her reply: "I said to you at the time that your answer helped me decide that you could be trusted, and nothing you've done since—though there's been a lot of stuff that's happened—has dissuaded me from that opinion. I want to thank you for that." He took this interchange as evidence that he was accepted in the college "as the kind of leader I want to be in terms of really pushing this idea of integrity."

His self-confidence has, of course, been reinforced by the philanthropic and enrollment successes of his tenure. These successes have apparently granted him a widening reputation for presidential prowess. At the time of the interview, he was relishing several invitations to make himself available for a third presidency, and he was presenting as his chief credential for them, not the enrollment or philanthropic achievements, but the "deep gladness" that he derived from his own integrity and the college's acknowledgement that it had acquired a good supply of this integrity in turn.

The Joy of Being Called

As continues to be true of all serious explorations of vocation, Frederick Buechner's definition quickly achieved orthodox status in the program's seminars.[2] The association of vocation with a "place," a place where one's "deep gladness" meets the world's "deep need," time and again beats all available rivals for conciseness and compact complexity.

With respect to the complexity, consider how differently the four cases just presented illustrate Buechner's definition. The first president searched for his "deep gladness" in acute self-awareness. In general terms, his gladness turned out to be effective service to his self-awareness. He learned that people who are self-knowing confess before their friends their uncertainty and self-doubt and therefore can undertake lives of public service to which they bring the full panoply of their talents. It is this "full employment" of one's self that this president and his spouse think of as "deep gladness."

The second of these four presidents hoped to find in his first presidency, by way of envisioning, a similar alignment of self and mission for himself and his spouse. But for the time being he found his gladness instead in helping his college assemble the makings of an institutional narrative that could, by another president, be processed into a distinctive and animating vision. In sum, this president imagined a community of thoughtful, interactive friends in which he and his spouse could freely and lovingly participate. In the meantime he served, duty bound, a deserving employer whose future he was confident could be made bright by an appropriate successor.

The third found his gladness in reaffirming with the help of his friends and presidential peers the vocational discernment of his youth, thus securing the purity of his life purpose from the centrifugal forces

---

2. Frederick Buechner, *Wishful Thinking: A Theological ABC* (New York: Harper & Row, 1973), 95.

of the workaday presidency. The life purpose that required such regular reaffirmation was to bring the immense blessings of enlightenment to the young and not-yet-lost scions of a culture busily embracing various forms of personal isolation and self-indulgence.

The fourth found gladness by living according to his deepest personal convictions and leading his college to do the same, first by his own example and then by providing instruction drawn from the college's own history and circumstance.

Life and work that accord with one's self-awareness, a duty-bound leadership that creates a community that embraces the leader as a friend, a determined campaign to bring the blessing of learning into a culture that is increasingly unwilling to embrace it, and an insistence on a brutal form of honesty that compels a college to live according to its mission: these constitute the gladnesses of four deeply reflective presidents who participated in the program and found much in the idea of vocation to recommend it.

To the degree that Buechner's definition is not only popular but also true, all vocationists have at some point experienced their own "deep gladness." But the definition supposes that one's reservoir of "deep gladness" is reached only through acts of service to the "world's deep need." It is not a pool of happiness from which the possessor can take a sip whenever his or her spirits flag. The fact that gladness is locked into a circuit with service and that service activates the circuit gives credence to the dialectical relationship between the vocationist and the world. Each is modified by the interaction. This idea illuminates the deeper meaning of "alignment." It isn't simply congruence of the president's vocation with the college's mission, or the college's mission with other aspects of the institution's management. It constitutes a synchronization that emerges from reciprocating contact. This aligning interaction plays a major role in sustaining the vocationist's commitment to his or her calling, simply because it alone can open the reservoir of deep gladness.

Vocational Resolve, Faith, and Education

The simultaneity of service and calling is playing out in the life and work of a dean and his wife who participated in the program from a Christian college. The spouse is a biologist. She is responsible for confronting believing first-year students mostly from rural families with Darwin's *The Voyage of the Beagle* and the idea of evolution.

Her own Christianity survived formal training in the sciences and is gaining new strength and sophistication from her annual presentation of the idea of evolution to freshmen, many of whom are the first in their families to go to college. Her strength and sophistication grow from the teaching itself and, even more, from her construction of a defense of this teaching against the frequent parental charge that it is blasphemy. To this charge, her first response is prudential: "If your child is to become the successful professional for whom you pray, he or she must be familiar with the idea of evolution and with the practices and concepts of experimental science."

Her second answer is fully vocational: the duty of the Christian college is to form self-consciously Christian professionals for lives of useful service in a fallen world. And it is here that she and the college itself meet the most serious challenge that vocationism poses for the faithful. Her questioners ask, "Doesn't your teaching of evolution amount to advocacy of evolution, and is not your advocacy of evolution proof that you have 'conformed to this world' instead of doing what is 'good and acceptable and perfect' in God's view?"—a paraphrase of language from Paul's letter to the Romans (12:2).

Speaking for her own work as well as the college's mission, she answers: "By teaching our students the ways of the world, we are helping to make them serviceable in it!" In her own view, she is "educating the faith" of her students so that they can sustain a more nuanced life of service. Both she and the dean see themselves as honoring through education Paul's encomium in Romans 12:6–8 RSV: "Having gifts that differ according to the grace given to us, let us use them: if prophecy, in proportion to our faith; if service, in our serving; he who teaches, in his teaching; he who exhorts, in his exhortation; he who contributes, in liberality; he who gives aid, with zeal; he who does acts of mercy, with cheerfulness."

For both the dean and the biologist, only an educated faith can survive the radical exposure to this world that vocation entails. Here we meet the biblical version of the "two worlds philosophy," the contrasting but related realms of law and of gospel. The dean, the biologist, and their colleagues all insist that exposure of their students to *this* world (the world of law rather than of gospel) be emphatically radical. They rail regularly against the propensity of premed students, for example, to pledge themselves exclusively to service in one or another foreign mission field. "You must remain alert to a call to practice in Manhattan," they point out, "or to lead a specialty at the Mayo Clinic." By "an educated faith" the couple means the armor that allows their students to go forth in service to the world without being corrupted by the world. They count on the immersion of their students in professional ethics during medical training and residency to complement the preparatory work of the college. Hence, they see profession as a handmaiden to vocation rather than a rival of it.

The dean and his biologist spouse cultivate this education of faith through a constant discernment conversation that involves the fundamental tension, for them, between faith and learning that is revealed by the commitment to vocation. "Interpreting the scriptural directive to be in the world but not of it by hanging out with your own kind," said the dean, "is non-vocational. It's fear-based, individualistic, and isolationist. In order to get our students to be genuinely vocational, we must get them over their fear of understanding"—as the world, rather than scripture, defines it.

Stories of these efforts, told over and again in their daily discernment discussions, reveal a "gladness" that consists in forming vocationists of true believers by demonstrating both abstractly and through the example of their own lives the reconciliation of faith and learning. This process began and continues to lift the students' faith off the pylons of habituated belief and tempers it by the freshening winds of freedom and responsibility. The couple's efforts have increased both their professional utility and their joint discipleship. Indeed, they are beginning to attract inquiries from executive search firms, and this reassures them that, far from laboring with marginal skills in a doctrinaire backwater, their work is the equal of anyone's in highly selective institutions, whether Christian or not.

Their confidence is crucial to the sustenance of personal vocational energy as well as to genuine inquiry into institutional mission. But the dean and his spouse are quick to deny that this particular kind of confidence constitutes pride. Indeed, they suggest that it insulates institutional mission from the corrupting and dissipating currents unleashed by a naive vocationism that simply "loves the world." Hence, the dean and his biologist spouse confess their need of practical virtue as a renewable resource for the sustenance of the mission they and their college are pursuing.

This couple came to the seminar to extend their discernment in the presence of peers they did not know. They were thrilled to find that their own reflections about the tension between faith and learning were paralleled among their secular peers by the search for reconciliation of one's self with one's work.

The story of this couple adds strength to the conviction that knowing and pursuing one's vocation frees one from fear and uncertainty, from pulling one's punches in public service and civil deliberation, and from embarrassment in the presence of hope and idealism. And the native ground of this freedom seems to lie at or near the point where a person's own particular abilities are employed in an ameliorating service to the world.

Mediating Realism and Idealism in Vocationism

In order to render such service, the vocationist must be realistic. The use of a naïve model, whether from another world or this one, to audit the practices of real life has doomed many a presidency. (In fact, this response is what caused at least one of the premature failures cited in Chapter One.) If the vocationist is actually to succeed in improving the life of a community, the model that guides the effort must be reformist, not revolutionary, and it must project a recognizable image of the community so as to draw its members into the strategic work of self-realization. It must be at least as careful to build on realism as to draw on idealism.

A dean came to the program utterly mystified by his mentor's nomination of him as a prospective president. At the time, he dreamed exclusively of a pastoral career among the congregations of his denomination. But he and his wife were gratified by her full inclusion in the inquiry and by the discovery that each of them had much to say and hear in conversations with peers from very different backgrounds.

Staying in touch with his colleagues both during the seminar and after brought him about two years later to acknowledge a budding interest in the presidency. He granted that some of this new interest was precipitated by the sudden and unexplained termination of the president who had nominated him to the program, followed immediately by the equally abrupt appointment of a stranger as her replacement.

These developments plunged him as well as his colleagues into a sea of insecurity. The senior administrators had been subject to a protective paternalism. Now, they all became anxious observers, even rivals, of each other. How, they asked themselves, were each of them to proceed? Resign? Seek a position elsewhere? Try to find a place in the new regime—and, if so, how?

What the dean realized was that he had not really collaborated with his colleagues—nor they with him—during his mentor's tenure. If he was to find a secure and useful place in the new order or to seek with confidence a new berth elsewhere in case he couldn't, he realized that he would have to develop effective working relationships with those who were not his friends. He reports that his self-confidence has risen dramatically, a change confirmed by his spouse, since he began engaging peers as co-workers rather than as secret rivals. Hence, he has elicited a level of collaboration among the group of administrators that has raised both the effectiveness of their collective work and his interest in it.

He claims, moreover, that this realpolitik engagement in the life of the college has given him, as he puts it, "a deeper sense of God's presence" in his life. When I asked him to explain this more fully, he reminded me that his discovery of cooperative instincts in himself and his colleagues was far more encouraging for his vocationism than leading praise and worship liturgies. "I am finding my new hope," he said, "in the reality that I had for so long feared and shunned." He is now harboring a new love of life. His spouse testifies that he has emerged from the experience kinder, gentler, more resolute, and lighter of heart. Once wondering why his mentor had nominated him, he is now assessing with a touch of impatience his own rising capacity and readiness for a presidency. Two years after we had last met, the dean and his spouse credit their revitalization to his deepened engagement in the give and take of civil society.

The dean's reflections upon collaborating with his colleagues (as both he and they see it), in a broken world, amounts to what might be called a "contextual theology." This theology has led him into engagement with the immediate world. He claims to find the divine in the midst of the mundane and he (like the biologist dean) revels in the utility of his service in this world. This orientation qualifies him as a vocationist.

Success as Sustenance for the Vocational Presidency

This dean's rising ambition for a vocational presidency is subjecting him to other beguiling aspects of the profane world, a world that he serves but to which he refuses to conform. He is showing, for example, a new appreciation of marketing, an art that vocational life requires but that some Christians and many academics find shameful.

A participant in an early program seminar had been appointed from a senior faculty position in the Ivy League to the presidency of an urban college that had made a fetish of a modesty rooted in its denominational identity. When he arrived to take up his duties, his new colleagues proudly told him, "We are the best kept secret in town!" He interpreted this remark as bad news and set out immediately to displace it with an aggressive marketing campaign. As a lifelong member of his new employer's sponsoring denomination, he appreciated and to some extent shared the modesty that had become imbued from the church into the college. Removing this attitude from the culture of the college without disturbing its legitimate role in the denomination led him to launch an envisioning effort at the institution that began with a reprise of the two-worlds philosophy on which the denomination had founded its earthly mission.

Both the enthusiasm with which he approached this task and the joy he received from its accomplishment are suggested by a recollection he shared during the interview. He discovered among the presidents in his program seminar another Ivy League leader who had also gone off to an urban college that had a diverse student population. Each asked the other about the incidence during their ten-to-twelve-year professorial tenures of student expressions of gratitude for a life-changing experience, either to them personally or to these urban institutions. Between them, one Ivy League graduate student came to mind who had said, "Thanks to you and thanks to this university for opening to me new worlds of beauty and opportunity that I had no idea even existed. You have not merely changed my life; you've given me new life!" Both then agreed that such testimony comes to them, as presidents of colleges with many first-generation and low-income students, much more frequently than it ever did in the Ivy League.

Even though both of these presidents are communicants of denominations that cultivate humility as a virtue, neither has the slightest hesitation in featuring transformative education as the distinguishing achievement of the colleges they lead. Both therefore regard their colleges as superior to the Ivies on this critical measure, and they regard their presidencies as providing a greater opportunity to educate students than did their tenured professorships. Both miss the well-read, articulate, and self-confident students they knew as scholar-teachers in their Ivy days, but they are confident that those students got much less of them—to say nothing of the institution—than their charges now do in these accessible urban institutions.

Hence, one of the realities of vocational life is that it is sometimes obscured by the modesty of its practitioners. The gift of a transformative education to one who never dreamed of its existence, to say nothing of expecting to receive it, is as energizing to the provider as it is to the individual student. It is energizing partly because the delivery of such a gift requires the full employment of the provider's ability, a practical understanding of competitive realities in the marketplace, and competence in the practice of marketing and other arts of modern management.

Sustaining this effort requires something more than the able practice of certain competencies. It also requires more than the knowledge that one has employed one's talent and energy fully and completely. The testimony of the participants in the Presidential Vocation and Institutional Mission Program suggests that the sustaining source for the hard work of the vocational presidency is the emergence in the college of a more hospitable learning community and of constituents who embrace that community when they otherwise might have remained committed to their own individual interests. This is the only really satisfying reward for work that is undertaken self-consciously as service.

A president with legal training reported during one interview that he pays no attention to his contract and has never hired a lawyer to negotiate it for him.

> If the board—for good reason or political whim—decides to get rid of you, they'll get rid of you. But I have my vocation, my self-confidence. And if things don't work out for me in this case or that, I'm naïve enough to say, 'I'll take the experience I've gained here, add it to what I learned earlier, and offer it where a better fit exists for me with my employer.'

His wife then added, "And we'll do there and then what we can to make ourselves pretty much indispensable!" For them, vocation fulfills their need to establish a sense of inner home.

Mentoring Networks

This latter president and his spouse believed that the presidency itself, because of the isolating effect of its perceived rank, prevents the kind of trustful sharing upon which mentoring depends. But the program provided a substitute: "Our seminar group became a mentor for us. We were all pretty much on each other's side. Together, we created a safe zone in which we could provide a mentoring role for each other. And I think it happened because we couldn't really get that for ourselves on campus."

That the seminars functioned as mentoring networks instead of as formal academic sessions means that the conversations they inspired were mutually advisory, mutually reassuring, and ultimately self-discovering, all aspects of a successful and productive mentoring relationship.

Many of the ideas presented in this chapter came to articulate form among participants in the course of the program. Between seminar meetings, participants tried new ideas in their various presidencies and reported their experiences to the group or in the interviews. One result has been this book, which grew from extensive conversations that went beyond the program and into the lives and practices of those who participated. The thinking that occurred in these conversations, the experiences that were remembered in them, and the enlightenment engendered in them were recorded in four hundred pages of transcripts from which the book is distilled.

Conclusion

A general outcome from this chapter's testimony is that, however limited might be the academic polity attempted by the vocational president, constructive work is guided by the vocationist's particular image of "community." Whether that model is taken from another world or this one, it can be inspiring only to the degree that it is both proximate to and accessible from the nominal realities on the campus. The president's perseverance in this work is sustained by friendship and mentoring that facilitate a regular concourse between himself or herself and each of these two worlds. It is in the nexus of this dialectic wherein lies the "deep gladness" that marks the center of the vocationist's life, whether in a presidency, elsewhere in the world of occupation, or even in retirement.

Having examined the definition of the vocational presidency and considered the role of envisioning in prior chapters, it is now time to describe the generic learning community toward which vocational presidents seek to move their colleges and universities.

CHAPTER 4

The Design and Construction of the Vocational College

Has the rise of vocationism among presidents and deans created a new category of American colleges and universities defined not so much by the number of students and the range of programs as by the patterns and purposes of administration, curriculum, pedagogy, and governance? Is there, in short, such a thing as "the vocational college"?

The best way to answer this question is to ask the presidents and deans who participated in the Presidential Vocation and Institutional Mission Program what they are doing in their own colleges, how they are doing it, and whether they think it's working. These are different questions from those we have pursued so far: What prompts their interest in academic leadership? What do they get out of it? How do they sustain their commitment to the work? And what impact did the program have upon their lives and their presidencies?

Before turning to the thirty-five responses of the presidents and deans who participated in the program, one must confess the difficulty in distinguishing vocational presidents and deans from non-vocational ones. After all, vocationists come in all shapes and sizes. The same is true of vocational colleges. Presidents, whether or not vocationists, celebrate the things that differentiate their institutions rather than the things they hold in common.

Just because this task is difficult doesn't mean that it cannot be done. Note, however, that one axiom that makes it impossible to identify vocationists in a crowd is that any imaginable undertaking can be a vocation. Until we confront and defeat that view, the particularity of vocation for leaders and institutions is lost, along with the credibility of claims concerning its advantages for public and personal life.

Frederick Buechner confronts this view in the essay in which he defines vocation as "the place where your deep gladness and the world's deep hunger meet." In the process of distinguishing vocations from the callings of society, superego, or self-interest, he introduces the notion of vocation as burden:

> The kind of work God usually calls you to is the kind of work
> (a) that you need most to do and (b) that the world most needs
> to have done. If you really get a kick out of your work, you've
> presumably met requirement (a), but if your work is writing
> cigarette ads, the chances are you've missed requirement (b).
> On the other hand, if your work is being a doctor in a leper
> colony, you have probably met requirement (b), but if most of the
> time you're bored and depressed by it, the chances are you have
> not only bypassed (a), but probably aren't helping your patients
> much either. Neither the hair shirt nor the soft berth will do.[1]

No college presidency of lasting tenure is a "soft berth." Indeed, many presidencies, especially those of abruptly foreshortened tenure, have been veritable hair shirts and made of the roughest imaginable material. Still, not every sustained and successful presidency is vocational, and for reasons that go beyond their failing to fall solidly between Buechner's

---

1. Buechner, *Wishful Thinking*, 95.

a and *b* categories. The decisive difference between those that are and those that aren't vocational rests not in the relative strenuousness of the work but in the nature of the vision the work serves. The vocational president is pledged to a communitarian image of the college. Like all visions, however, that of the vocational president awaits realization; it is, by definition, an image yet to be realized in its fullest form because the president discovers it from cultivating and engaging friends of the college at all levels. Transforming the vision into reality and acknowledging the ongoing modifications of that image is a kind of midwifery sustained by the "deep gladness" of effective service to the envisioned college.

The challenge is to hold onto the principle that vocations constitute a distinctive genus of commitments and undertakings without unduly constricting the range of communitarian forms that are species in that genus. My challenge here is to bring into sufficient focus various vocational colleges that the program's participants lead and nurture without breaching the anonymity promised in the interviews and without creating disorder from the multi-facetedness of those interviews.

The definitive purpose of the vocationists described in this chapter is, on the one hand, to develop persons who can escape futures severely restricted by poverty, limited learning or physical disabilities, and the like. On the other, the purpose is to fend off the debilitating effects of a cosseting and isolating affluence. They are readied for this work by widened literacy and contextual sensitivity and by having learned to serve others from the service they have received. Their loyalty runs first to community and thence to the self.

From Administration to Vision in the Revitalization of an Undergraduate College

A presidential couple came to the program from a successful seven-year tenure, wondering whether to work up new tasks for the existing presidency or to look for another with more pressing need of their experience and talent. Both president and spouse credited the development and disciplined operation of the college's administrative apparatus as the principal instrument of the president's success.

Among their several accomplishments, they noted two in particular: the articulation for marketing and governing purposes of a new rationale for the college's strictly undergraduate liberal arts curriculum, one that reconciled the founding purposes of the school with its modern condition and circumstance; and linkage of the college with business, public service, and arts organizations adjacent to the campus to found a new political community in which the college was a full partner.

They described the process that produced the new raison d'etre for the curriculum as "transformative," not of the curriculum (it didn't change) but of the institution. It was the president's idea and it entailed revision of the somewhat tattered relationship between the college and its sponsoring church, a new emphasis on vocation and vocational thinking in the curriculum, and encouragement that faculty bring "faith considerations" into the classroom as both support for and counterpoint to reason.

It was novel for this college to forge an alliance with service and arts organizations in the surrounding neighborhoods of the campus in the effort to form a civil society. Yet, it was all but dictated by the new rationale for the college's curriculum that declared liberal education as the "only practical education for life in a free society," the central promise of the college's founders a century earlier.

In the process of recovering this rationale, both president and college came to agree that the modern rise of professional education had somehow broken into the heart of liberal education and stolen away its original practicality. This great theft had left the liberal arts divided into increasingly isolated and specialized departments and therefore disengaged from professional and entrepreneurial life, except as the suppliers of writing and speaking skills useful in marketing or other presentations. Getting this strictly undergraduate liberal arts college back in touch with the real world of business, the professions, and the social interactions of community without adding professional studies programs seemed imperative in the president's experience. Engaging the college directly with its immediate neighborhoods struck the president and his spouse as the best way to start.

As they revealed their thinking with facilitators and peers in the seminar program and reviewed the liberal education rationale and the civil society initiative it was to spawn, they began to see themselves as extending the vocational presidency that they earlier suspected had run its course. Indeed, their consideration of these matters in the context of the program, with its constant reference to the terms and conditions of vocation, helped them to see that their work had amounted to much more than clarification of the college's mission. Even though neither the college's enrollment and residential profile nor its curriculum changed much in form, each began to seem a defining attribute of institutional purpose rather than a mere mark of recognition. The college's pride in itself became palpable, according to the president, and his and his wife's sense of accomplishment reinvigorated their interest in the potential of the place.

Coming to the presidency as a non-academic professional, the president had never personally experienced the kind of liberal education the college offered. But one of his children had done so in a similar setting; so had his spouse. The president admired the learning each had acquired, and was deeply gratified by the moral and ethical proclivities it had cultivated in the offspring. Having become a partisan of the college's curriculum in the process of searching for the new rationale, the president concluded during the Presidential Vocation and Institutional Mission Program that the defense and promotion of the liberal arts had become his vocation. Developing the implications of his commitment in the life of that particular college would become the work of this commitment to the institution.

This president and his spouse came to the program, therefore, thinking that administration and vocation were two peas in a pod of the college and university presidency. In this view, the distinguishing initiatives of any particular presidency are simply those guided by best practices as adapted to local conditions. During the seminar inquiry, both confirmed a principal attribute of vocation in colleges and universities: if the vision that rationalizes critical features of the institution is drawn in part from its saga, and in part from the modern world's "deep needs," the college's financial health and market attractiveness will naturally improve, and the institution's general morale will probably rise proportionally. The rationale that the president assembled for the liberal arts from the college's saga and from persuasive diagnoses of the current economy's human resource needs strengthened the college's defense of its curriculum against the corrosive effects of fields-of-study specialization and value relativism. If neither the president nor the college is eventually guided by purposes other than those that they simply inherit and therefore accept, they shall be denied the joy of vocational life. That is the joy of transcendence. Moving from one station of self-awareness to a higher one can also lead to increased self-awareness, which, in this case, seems to have occurred. The president's original wonderment about "what next, and where" became "what next here" and "where else eventually."

The president is now pursuing reforms meant to bring the college closer to the model and at a pace kept just at the edge of that which is acceptable to its modern constituents. Moreover, the conversations of this couple during the seminar with each other and with their peers, and their experience in applying the lessons of vocation to their work have put them at peace with what was once a profoundly unsettling conclusion, namely that that both the reforms and the vision they serve are inevitably modified in the process of realization.

Vocation as a Faculty Development Strategy in an Undergraduate College

The provost of another strictly undergraduate liberal arts college decided during his participation in the program to stick with his position because he was finding profound satisfaction in bringing the faculty into congruence with the president's effort to deepen the college's dedication to liberal education. It was, in fact, the excellence of his leadership that had convinced the president to nominate the provost to the program. It was the program, in turn, that helped the provost to recognize his own acumen in leading the faculty.

In the interview, the provost remembered his and the president's effort to move the faculty course load from five to four. "This department liked it; that one didn't. This person feared that it would degrade the college's reputation and that one thought it would enhance it. We were really stuck," he said.

"We decided to convene a series of faculty lunches to break the logjam, but all we heard was what we were doing wrong." The provost interpreted this immobilization as his and the president's failure to translate the core mission of the college into what he called "an academic vision" that might capture the imagination of the faculty. To accomplish this translation, he developed a history of the college's effort "to become a full-fledged liberal arts college." This account succeeded in "bringing us all back to our common elements" and in locating the course load issue at a certain juncture in a long and continuing saga.

The provost then used the authority generated by his putting the issue into the context of the college's central story to resolve it. "There comes a point," he said, "when you say, 'Okay! We've looked at this and we know it will be a problem for some of us, but it's going to be in the best interest of the college. So, we're going to do it this way or that!' I'm sure," he said of his decision, "that several of the critics didn't like the decision or the way it was made. But I know that a good number of them said, 'Thank God! Now we know what we're going to do, and we don't have to debate it anymore.'"

While preparing together for and then participating fully in the seminar inquiry, the provost and his wife, who was an elementary school teacher, came to appreciate the powerful influence of the college in each of their lives. This influence, they agreed, was not as a home in which they dwelt contentedly, but a project that drew them out of themselves and into a deep engagement with and love of life. They noticed, for example, that the provost had developed an especially valuable talent for "mediating the internecine squabbles of the faculty." "If you give me a word or math problem," he said, "I'll work on it for a couple of minutes. Then I'll look up the answer in the back of the book. But if you give me a personnel problem, especially a faculty personnel problem, I'll work on it until I solve it."

He approaches these problems as a chess game in which he "must think three or four moves ahead." As he put it recently to an interviewer for a professional journal, "I really think that my job is not about imposing a vision that comes down from me or from the president. It's about working with people to craft a vision that they can own, because that vision has to be congruent with who they are." He is confident of finding such congruencies "because I've learned a secret about faculty in my college: they think they are independent spirits, each very different from every other. But I intersect with them all the time in different meetings and settings, and I know that each one of them has at heart a vision that he or she picked up from each other during their time in the college. I've learned how to help them commune with one another as they craft that underlying vision' and bring it into view. "This process is chaotic," he says. "The faculty doesn't think they have a shared vision. But I think they do, and the trick is to bring that truth into view without insulting their sense of independence."

When a dispirited faculty member tells him, "I don't feel like I belong here," the provost's "secret" allows him to respond: "Tell me, what is the 'here' you prefer, because there are multiple 'heres' here!" Vocation obliges its adherents, he points out, to "find your place" in a community made of many vocations, none of which exists at any moment or in any real sense outside of community.

One of the reasons that this provost trusts his faculty, and they him, is that he has for years recruited its members by presenting the college as "an institution that aspires" and which therefore seeks "builders" rather than those who are looking for a place that has been built. He claims that it has been this invitation to join in defining and advancing the mission of the college, rather than the offer of opulent contracts or the provision of personal research facilities, that has raised the quality and credentials of the college's faculty.

The Relationship in Vocational Colleges between the Instrumental and Envisioned Regimes

Because the visions that orient aspiring colleges are always becoming and never finished, the maintenance of their credibility requires a special kind of husbandry. What needs tending is the relationship between the ends and the means, between the vision, on the one hand, and the initiatives that serve it, on the other.

What seems to be needed for keeping ends and means both vibrant and mutually consistent is attentive concern for baseline institutional health. If there is no particular reason to worry about declining enrollment, increasing attrition, operational and financial-aid expenses that are outpacing revenue, and rising levels of deferred maintenance, or if a general spirit of contentment is afoot in the college, it is unlikely that vocationist presidents will be chosen or get a chance to practice the envisioning arts for long.

A dean-become-president set out to restore to his college its original denominational identity. He had concluded from his discernment reflections in the Presidential Vocation and Institutional Mission Program that he would feel most at home in a strictly undergraduate, financially solid, religiously affiliated college. But he found himself passing up several such opportunities. They didn't seem to need him. Eventually, he accepted an appointment to the presidency of a troubled institution that possessed a noble but half-forgotten church-related educational tradition.

To figure out whether and how the tradition might be recovered and what advantage the recovery might bring to the financial welfare of the college, he commissioned interviews of 250 members of the campus community, including faculty, staff, alumni, and students. As he hoped, the interviews showed that the college's competitive advantage was its denominational identity, however weakened by neglect. But they also showed that the salient demand of students in the region was for professional-studies programs for both undergraduate and graduates.

The president had long been convinced that professors of science are more faithful than professors of the humanities. Scientists, he thought, tend to stand in awe of their subjects whereas humanities professors often demystify and presume to master their subjects. He reasoned that if scientists, of all people, could hold onto faith in the crucible of their research and scholarship, the college could certainly reconcile its denominational identity with the incorporation of professional studies programs in its undergraduate curriculum. Hence, he set out to resuscitate and sharpen the institution's denominational identity as the crucial first step in meeting the regional demand for professional education.

Not unexpectedly, many faculty resisted the president's effort to recover the educational philosophy of the college's founders. The critics had cast their courses in molds supplied by their graduate training and were convinced that the college's founding philosophy was both out-dated and compromised by religious considerations. Moreover, much of the faculty imagined the college to be "highly selective" and didn't want this sacrificed to the accessibility they saw lurking in the strategy for denominational recovery.

The president mined the college's competitive situation as best he could to keep the recovery strategy going. He pointed out that a peer college, competing in that same regional market, had strayed even far-ther from its sectarian roots than had the president's institution. He observed that, in doing so, the competitor had found new markets in which to compete effectively and so had gained new viability. But that college had thereby abandoned the very regional and immediate market segment at which the president's recovery strategy was aiming.

He observed that public institutions in the region were taking up the slack, but he doubted that they could continue to do so. After all, he argued, they were using their tuition price subsidies to recruit the most highly qualified students in the market—and then disappointing them with huge classes, low and slow graduation rates, and anti-concentration general education requirements. He concluded that his college could capitalize on its distinctive denominational self-definition and thereby recruit a good number of students that had been effectively abandoned by the private segment of the market. By adding undergraduate and graduate professional programs that were especially respectful of both religious and ethical considerations, the college could compete directly and effectively with the public institutions.

All in all, this combination of market diagnosis and envisioning gave the president the purchase he needed to propel the college into full-dress vocationism. None of this—including the revolutionary turn toward accessibility—could have been accomplished without the dete-riorating condition of the college, on the one hand, and the atrophied sectarian identity lying fallow in the institution's history, on the other.

Early on in this envisioning effort, before it was vindicated by rising enrollment and financial surpluses, one may have heard on this president's campus the kind of critical remarks that are ubiquitous on American campuses under similar circumstances:

> See, the president: a) is reneging on the promise of higher salaries and a lower faculty workload, b) has changed his mind yet again, c) is naïve, d) has been captured by a rival constituency that never really bought into the envisioning stuff anyway. He or she therefore should resign, give up on those new program initiatives or that branch campus, hire Joe and Mary as co-provosts and turn over management of the faculty entirely to them, or be fired for leading us away from "who we are."

Though this president didn't face so full a range of criticism, he met enough to require adjustments. He treated these adjustments as "revisions" of his various reforms—alterations that were consistent with the vision. Moreover, they were absolutely *required* by the "institutional culture" of the college. Here, he meant, not "the vision and mission" of the college but "the mediating, administrative mores of the college." This instrumental regime, as we might call it, "gets the business done," he said. "It creates the conversations among the faculty that ultimately legitimize the changes; it interprets them as driven by the mission and vision."

Maintaining Authority for Vocational Leadership while Accomplishing Reform

Shepherding the authority the president needed for reform was further complicated in this case by the institution's new commitment to increased access. The shift caused by this new commitment produced dramatic growth in both enrollment and employment and required the use of new pedagogies to handle the "barbell" profile among students, where some well-prepared students were offset by an equal number of others barely beyond remedial need. Faculty reported that such changes made them feel "less connected" to the college.

The president and his spouse reacted by "starting all kinds of things" to reconnect them: a monthly all-campus meeting, a general initiative to deepen religiosity and widen the hospitality of the denominational tradition, and a campaign to acknowledge the contributions of staff to the education of students by including them in commencement and other exercises. Although the staff has greeted the good progress on each of these initiatives with enthusiasm, the faculty, says the president, continue to "feel as though they've lost something" in the more fully integrated campus community and in the shift of institutional self-image from high selectivity to wide accessibility.

The president uses every rhetorical opportunity to establish consistency with the vision of these unexpected and sometimes unwelcome changes. In a chapel homily about the story of the prodigal son delivered the morning of the interview, he had compared the social-justice rationale of his faculty critics (who pressed for more commitment to economic needs in the community) with the denominational one recovered from the founding. Quoting theologian Henri Nouwen's remarks about the complaint of the prodigal's dutiful brother, the president argued that "in God's economy, you discover that your sense of fairness, your sense of justice, is not necessarily his." Hence, he concluded, social justice as a this-world creation of human reason unmodified by the insights of faith could not embrace the prodigal or restore him to the family. Likewise, he said, the college without its denominational rationale could not offer a warm enough hospitality to the diverse array of strangers it was recruiting.

Vocational Commitment and Personal Experience

To bring a college into alignment with itself, a vocational president must paint and display the model for the enterprise before the college.

It cannot simply be located or pointed out because it doesn't really exist in historical terms. It is created from the institution's founding, its traditions or saga, and its current setting and circumstance. It is vision, not construct; orientation, not destination; a state to be preferred, not experienced. It constitutes an identity that has yet to be realized. When its authority is secure and growing, it commands the attention and orients the hopes of both the president and the college.

But what draws the vocational president to the vision and elicits from him or her the gladdening effort to bring a college closer to its highest potential?

Vocational enthusiasm often grows directly from a transformative learning experience. For those who credit the biggest steps in their own self-knowledge to learning important things about someone or something else, any subsequent introduction to vocation precipitates an instant sense of familiarity. Consider the testimony of a president who felt called at midlife to a denominational college that had been overwhelmed by the demand for learning from the economically and culturally deprived residents of its urban neighborhood.

His own undergraduate experience had "profoundly changed my life, my understanding of myself, and what I believed I was set on earth to do." He had encountered "the greatest pleasures of my life" in academe. These were certainly not the pleasures of peace and contentment. Indeed, he was fascinated to hear from several of his colleagues in the Presidential Vocation and Institutional Mission Program that they were at peace with themselves. He doubted that vocationists were ever "at ease with themselves."

Like many vocationists, he had never felt so. Indeed, he thinks that "the part of our lives in which we are *not* at peace with ourselves is the home of our doubts, on the one hand, as well as our aspirations and hopes, on the other." He wonders whether those who live with "the illusion of certainty" are actually enjoying themselves. He is clear that he doesn't want himself or his college ever to be content and satisfied with the status quo.

So what is his college's vocation? "To serve students," he said; "to invite them to come and find their best selves." The college had had "immense problems" in rendering this service and "over years of adversity had lost its self-confidence." Nevertheless, it had attracted an extraordinarily strong faculty. It was this faculty, in concert with predilections conferred by his own history and training, that led him to accept the appointment.

He had been raised in a working-class Eastern city. From this background of practical wisdom and worldly intelligence, he came upon liberal education and discovered in it "the best preparation, bar none, for the world of work." Indeed, his college was a portal of access to this world for every one of its students.

This background and educational philosophy, as well as his readiness to engage a strong but beleaguered faculty, worked together to defend liberal arts education for a student body half of whom were first-generation and from the inner city. The work was exciting and created a new sense of self-possession in the college.

He told a story of his own efforts and those of the college to enroll and graduate an inner-city boy who reminded him, he said, of his own grandfather. The grandfather had been indentured in his native Ireland. The inner-city boy had been raised by a single mother in a tough neighborhood. The president had hoped to help this student as his grandfather had helped him. The student's mother had seen to it that he came to college with a solid high school education, but he arrived at college recovering from a shooting. Within a semester, he had flunked out.

The president knew enough about the boy to ask for the file. He saw promise in the transcript, suspected that the college had not succeeded in getting the boy over his fear of higher education, and invited the boy and his mother to come in for a visit. He wondered whether he could get the boy to try school again. Although an appointment was arranged for that purpose, neither the student nor his parent showed up. The president had hoped to deliver a warm invitation to the student to return to college life and offer him a place in college organizations in order to allay the possible fears the president believes precipitated the student's sense of isolation.

Superficially, this president's commitment to making his college accessible to a diverse student population is indistinguishable from that of the presidents of the great majority of smaller private colleges. So what does his vocationism add, if anything, to this widely shared commitment? The story of this president's relentless effort to enroll, educate, and graduate the promising survivor of urban gun violence suggests the answer. He thinks of himself as saving students for citizenship in a yet-to-be-realized polity. The president believes that without his effort and that of his college, many more would be lost than now are to illiteracy, thoughtlessness, and indulgence in the dissipating forces of popular culture. He is trying with all his might to proffer an uncompromised liberal education to students up against such challenges despite the expense of higher education and other factors, even though he knows that the student beneficiaries will have almost no immediate interest in it. In fact, he is trying to do for his students what was done for him in his youth.

This is more than supplying opportunity to those who might not otherwise have it; more than creating a level playing field; more, even, than providing a platform for self-expression in a culture that assumes that each of us is potentially creative. It constitutes commitment to a community in which each member can find his or her better self—*through* service to the community.

The Ministry of the Vocational President and of the Vocational College

The interviews suggest that this high level of service cannot be sustained without a personal experience enshrining liberal education as the best preparation for *both* employability and good living. In any event, every president with whom I spoke who reported such an experience sponsored a first-year program seeking the immediate engagement of students in the public life of the college; sought a literate, thoughtful, and caring faculty; pushed for a high discount rate funded in part by a demandingly aggressive annual fund and deferred gift campaigns; and offered tutoring and counseling programs that maintain the line between introductory collegiate and remedial work without denigrating and demoralizing those who require the latter.

Indeed, the president at the center of this account calls his work a ministry, the prerequisite of which is accessibility. Accessibility for him and for vocational presidents in general is not so much a strategy as the institutional purpose that orients strategy. It is no accident that such presidents are surrounded with examples of men and women of various ages accomplishing remarkable things in study and work, things that could only be expected of them in the encouraging context of the vocational college. Further, vocational presidents, whatever their religious stripe, put these examples forward as achievements of the college, not personal achievements, either of their own or of their colleagues.

Accessibility is a reiterated, almost universal claim of the institutional membership of the Council of Independent Colleges. But vocational presidents and colleges add a reformist element to what is often a strictly prudential institutional appeal to an underserved demographic stratum of demand for higher education. The president for whom accessibility is a ministry monitors his college's pledge to save promising people from a potential condition of unemployability and also a culture of individualism. In creating an atmosphere in which every notable achievement of this kind is celebrated and in which the college prospers as a result, the president is giving himself and his faculty a sustaining sense of fulfillment.

Work as the Redemption of Vocation and the Liberal Arts

The provost of a college that provides access to financially disadvantaged rural students by employing them on campus came to the program in his tenth year as dean of the faculty to consider whether he was qualified for and interested in a presidency. He eventually decided that he was both interested and qualified and has since been a finalist in three searches.

By way of conversations in his particular seminar of the Presidential Vocation and Institutional Mission Program, he realized that his college had given him experience in one of the axioms of vocational thinking—that liberal learning is to be applied directly to life. That is the very principle of his college's student-employment program. In fact, the principle was applied with such purity that the program was actually student managed.

The provost's greatest challenge in supervising this program and working with the students who manage it is to make sure that the learning conveyed by the faculty is, in fact, liberal learning and that it is this learning (and not training in job competency) that is being applied in the employment.

"What is exciting about the college is that we continue to creep toward better and more intentional integration of formal learning and experiential dimensions of student life." This slow but steady progress has opened a "remarkable opportunity" at the college "to build a community of the sort conceived by John Dewey—a truly democratic society in which learning and experience are woven together." That union, he believed, would increase the contribution of each kind of learning—experiential and traditional—to good as well as productive living.

He applies this thinking in his work with the faculty. "I try hard to bring people on board with this institutional vision," he says, and he draws the attention of his and the president's faculty critics to these matters when the relationship becomes especially adversarial. He reaffirms the common beliefs and attitudes that make shared governance both possible and effective. He believes that PhDs from prestigious graduate schools come to his college "because somewhere in the heart of what they're about are these core values of Dewey's dream, of work and life unified as can only be accomplished in a small, liberal arts college." These faculty, he says, "really want to teach, they want to be in a classroom, they want to work with students and mentor them, and they want to have colleagues of the same sort."

The provost quite consciously takes responsibility for cultivating the college's hospitality to such faculty. He says that he "almost always has a handful of mentoring projects ongoing—with a young department chair or perhaps with a new program director." These, he says, "are opportunities for me to provide new faculty with a safe setting for talking about their challenges and concerns. And," he said, "these projects give me an opportunity to help staff think about their own commitments and responsibilities, both to themselves and to the college's mission." He believes he has developed a special skill in this kind of mentoring, and has used the conversations to work out succession in the management of the college's academic divisions and programs.

He emphatically notices the intersection of his college's work-culture tradition and the service commitments of vocational life at the foot of the great tradition of liberal education. For him and for his faculty the only way to lift the college's students from poverty to citizenship, from isolating fear to lives called to service, is with the aid of a liberal arts tradition that respects the differences between and the mutual support of faith and reason. With these commitments solidly in hand, the college can provide a truly useful education to those who come wanting employability, but who lack initial interest in liberal education either because they are unaware of that tradition or critical of it.

This dean's vocational commitment embraces "transformative education"—a very familiar concept among vocationist presidents. Among other things, it means an education in which academic excellence and broad institutional accessibility can be reconciled and merged. It resists the conversion of education into job training and the exclusion of liberal studies from professional and preprofessional programs.

Taming Individualism: Discovering Independence in Community

The president of a radically egalitarian secular institution restored the college to its former glory by helping it find and appropriate a singular statement of its educational principles and an integrated strategy to guide its curricular and program development. As a friend of the college's original mission, he had been appointed to reverse a long decline in its fortunes. He discovered upon arrival that a recent accreditation visit had turned up on campus five different mission statements with varying levels of currency.

He concluded that the root cause of the confusion lay in the current understanding of the founding vision. That understanding seemed to suppose that a welcoming and sustainable learning community could be generated by assembling and liberating individuals to pursue their preferences and acquire wisdom in a highly permissible setting and without the sanctions of grades or tests.

Some of this naiveté had flowered in the college's turn toward convenient education for working adults, an alternative to the conventional three-day semester or five-day quarterly programs whose charm had faded in the wake of the American withdrawal from Vietnam. The decline continued and the naiveté grew. What had once been a scintillating array of international students became a small band of locals; what had once been a vibrant scene of debate and deliberation became a passive platform for the presentation of eccentricities.

All this suggested to the new president that a new relationship was needed between individual and community. Radical individualism, liberated and left to itself, would not produce a sustainable, self-governing community. "We are now trying to be," says the president, "an individualized community committed to the common good." He explains: "We continue to be built around the individual and his or her interests. But we are insisting that the individual does not develop a sense of responsibility except in the context of social reality and on behalf of social justice."

The president says that this message is proving very attractive to seven hundred to two thousand potential American college students in any specific year. Enrollment projections for the college could be much higher if it were to elaborate its convenience offerings, but doing so would risk the revitalization that the president has accomplished. "Short residency programs could lead to a degree a meal at a time. It is part of being radical," he says, "that the learning is rigorous. The faculty is invigorated by the new regime. There are no courses, so they are working one-on-one with students, and the stories of transformative learning are exhilarating. If you get me started on this, I'll go on and on about it; it's been a great time for me."

From Social Alienation to Vocational Commitment

The president's success in revitalizing this college lay in socializing the individualist principles of its mission. His extension of this critical reform by linking the socialized individualist to the common good by way of "social responsibility" pushed the revitalized (yet still radical) college toward civility.

The compelling sense of responsibility among vocational presidents to the discovery and promotion of the core identity of the colleges they lead makes them natural "refounders" of these institutions. As they pursue the alignment of the college's operational and rhetorical life with the institution's vision, they actually raise the reference point of the college's identity from its particular constituencies to its internal essence. This teleological process seeks to establish a community in the place of a collection of constituencies, a purpose in the place of an organizational form.

With the help of his peers, a particularly scholarly president came to the program to reflect upon the propriety of his effort to construct a modern vision for his college from its original founding. This president offered the seminar some very helpful linguistic enlightenment concerning vocation. He pointed out that the root of the German word which Martin Luther used for "vocation" is *ruf*, meaning "how we are known." *Beruf* thus means "the work by which we are known," and *berufung*, "the self-identifying work to which we are called."

This little lesson came to him at the point in which his own professional competencies met his presidential responsibilities. He was appointed by an institution that had intentionally and forthrightly shed its denominational origins in order to survive in a secular age and a particular market context. For him to give that college vocational vitality, he had to recover certain Christian concepts from the rubble of its rejected tradition, dress them in mufti and shepherd them across the border from the denominational to the generically secular.

"In this place, I am part of the process of human beings collectively becoming more articulate about what they do and about this particular institution," he said. "I am helping us toward a contemporary community, and that requires that we commune with our original self, so to speak. But if that is done in the actual terms of the founding vision, the chances of our becoming a community now will be lost; the faculty will say, 'Don't use those old ideas! We've rejected them.' And if I keep pushing those old ideas in their original form, they'll say, 'The new president doesn't understand us. He's not listening.'"

He explained that he looks for missional ideas among the strategies of the college's Christian founders, recasts them in secular language, and adapts them to the modern needs of the institution. Much of this work is done by rhetoric and, if successful, results in a commonly used message by representatives of the college to market, operate, and promote the institution. Rhetoric is both the creator and registry of the college's existence as a community.

It is very important to the authority of his presidency that credit for the college's sharpened self-awareness and the rising institutional financial health resulting from it go to his colleagues and the college. Even a hint that the ideas at the heart of this rejuvenating collegiate story originated in him, he thinks, imperils the project. The vision that is becoming clearer as the profile of the college improves must belong in every possible way to the institution itself.

The Role of the Liberal Arts in the Transformation of College into Polity

The little lesson concerning *ruf* suggests that the modern concept of vocation, from the moment of its birth in the Reformation, has been profoundly social and public, rather than asocial and private. The clearest example of an "antivocation" for the Reformers was monasticism because it took refuge from society instead of entering it. Indeed, both Luther and Calvin sought to root their revolutionary idea of vocation in new schools and colleges whose graduates were expected to apply the concept to the development of new forms of civil society that were already taking form to replace the rule of the church. Every reformer fully agreed with Phillip Melanchthon's statement that "to raise offspring for time to come . . . colleges should be instituted for instructing children, to prepare them for ministry as well as civil government."[2]

A president came to the program for guidance in convincing his deeply denominational college to offer "its curricular and pedagogical gifts" to the world instead of seeking to position itself as a moral and

---

2. Philip Melanchthon, *Orations on Philosophy and Education*, Sachiko Kusukawa, ed.; Christine F. Salazar, trans. (Cambridge, England: Cambridge University Press, 1999), 16–17, 29–53, 77, and *passim*.

religious bastion in the midst of a profane marketplace. As it first presented itself to him, the college appeared to be a cloistered religious order, sheltered by its pious modesty on the periphery of a vibrant urban environment. But a couple of other dimensions allowed it to tap into unmet local demand for funding the cloistered undergraduate core. Getting it ready for more sturdy service to the needs of the world, rather than to the narrower and more exclusive interests of the sponsoring church, meant reorganizing it to compete effectively in the higher education marketplace.

"We had taken the name of 'university,' but we hadn't taken the form," he said. "We had an undergraduate liberal arts school, a graduate school, and a school of professional studies that included degree-completion programs for working adults." This structure required three deans and their collateral administrations and three each of certain faculty specialties, such as psychology and business. "So we set this framework on its head. We organized the 'university' as a School of Education, a School of Business, a School of Natural Sciences, and a School of Humanities, Religion and Social Sciences." Faculty resisted these changes, both structural and cultural.

The president's ability to absorb criticism and sustain reform was rooted in his earlier experience in representing a university to a state legislature, in his credentials as a practicing member of the college's denomination, in his exploitation of the institution's "financial exigency," and in his candid and frequent communications with campus personnel.

His interpretation that the theology of the denomination obliged it to serve the world boldly was made credible by his scholarship and credentials. The community knew that the institution's financial health was failing, so the president presented the structural changes and cultural shift as an integrated extension of the college's founding mission *and* as its modern redemption. He made the reforms an actual envisioning process by using this diagnosis and redemptive promise in responding—directly and frequently—to criticism. He also traced any measurable improvement in the university's financial indicators to the realization of the vision and offered a weekly status report concerning the restructuring and cultural reorientation.

Criticism has not disappeared but it has diminished. Not all of the reforms worked, but enough did to assure improvement in the financial picture. More and more of the faculty are thrilled to be offering their learning to people who both need it and are grateful to be acquiring it.

This president sees four groups in the faculty, and he describes each of them in light of their varying capacities for "institutional civility." First are partisans of denominational purity. These are complainers and politicians who cite process concerns and alleged violations of the faculty handbook to stall, stop, or reverse decisions. Second are scholars—academic and professional—who quietly go on with their work so long as they are left free to do it as they please. This group is growing, which helps to accomplish his reforms, according to the president. The scholars embarrass and thereby isolate the politicians. But they don't easily form allies with the program and department chairs who hold the balance of influence in faculty governance. They're the ones the president expected to support the restructuring and culture shift. But the support came instead form the fourth group: the teachers. "All of our teachers of the year were in that group," he said. "That's where the next leaders will come from." (He didn't expect new "politicians" to rise from the group of teachers.)

Both the president and his wife credited the Presidential Vocation and Institutional Mission Program with helping them cope with the once cacophonous but now diminishing faculty criticism. The program validated what the president was doing and the way he was reporting it to the campus. It gave him the idea of vocation, long familiar as a personal matter, in the new form of institutional envisioning, which helped him reconcile his reforms of the university with the denominational principles of its founding.

The president felt emboldened by the seminar "to tell stories to the campus about the effect of the changes on the college (regarding student achievement or new institutional commitments). I can also tell stories about things that worry me or improvements that vindicate the effort." This kind of communication has made the president known to the campus in such immediate and candid terms that the rumors and other misrepresentations of his purposes and policies have trouble gaining traction. Increasingly, the president and his wife are hearing that the open-minded members of the community "know the president's heart."

Listening to the College in Constructing the Vision

This president relied upon his lifelong membership in and scholarly knowledge of the college's tradition and his diagnosis of its current circumstance to plan the realization of the institution's new identity as an engaged entity in civil society. He attended to the college's self-understanding only so that he could correct it. For resilience in the work, he referred to his own convictions, the support of his spouse and a small coterie of faculty leaders who were champions of the vision he had extracted by memory, scholarship, and diagnosis. As a result of all this, he himself was more or less untouched by the envisioning process that was visiting a steady stream of transforming effects upon the college. He thus used the denominational tradition itself to contribute principally to the new institutional self-definition.

In contrast, another president brought to the program a report that the envisioning process she initiated had been substantially redirected by the observation of a student. She had just concluded a strategic planning cycle that was intended, among other things, to help the college sharpen its mission. As a revised mission statement began to percolate up from the various drafting exercises of the planning process, she circulated it among several college constituencies. Eventually, a thoughtful and interested student observed in a forum considering one of these drafts, "That's not the college I'm attending!" That observation brought the planning process to a standstill and led the president to seek a redraft of the mission statement from the student and his peers.

The student's intervention set the process off in a positive direction. A little time later, the board authorized and the college embraced as its mission the provision of counseling and other resources to help students discern their particular vocations. They also launched a plan to revise the curriculum and improve the array of available programs to prepare students to successfully perform the work of their vocations.

The result gave the president a proprietary stake in the college's mission and plan. It connected her own encounter, during her recruitment to the presidency, with the idea of vocation. She had resisted repeated invitations to enter the search because of timing; it anticipated rather than matched her own established schedule and estimated readiness for the work. When the first search failed, she hesitated again to apply for candidacy. Her spouse, a pastor and himself a vocationist, asked a leading question that persuaded her to apply: "What part," he asked, "of being so obviously called to that presidency don't you understand?"

She heeded the call, and among the eventual achievements of her presidency were several which actually grew from the vocationist mission suggested by the students. Being able to convincingly trace strategic initiatives back to the vision is necessary to the legitimacy of both the initiative and the vision, but the generic character of strategic initiatives makes this difficult. After all, the initiatives that serve a vocational college in realizing its vision are often indistinguishable from those that a conventional college employs to recruit its enrollment or strengthen its balance sheet. Certainly, every prudent college should assemble a peer group to evaluate institutional performance, develop a comprehensive strategic plan (including a campus master plan), complete a market survey to identify the character and clarity of the institution's reputation, adopt structural reform to present the college consistently to the public, and specify in an academic master plan the programs and experiences that accomplish the educational objectives of the institution.

Although each of these focal points may have been undertaken to save the college by simply bringing it to heel administratively, this vocational president turned these generic tools toward drawing the constituents of the college into a shared understanding of what the college was trying to accomplish, and indeed, what the college was consciously trying to become.

A market survey and identification of an institutional peer group were not aimed at proving the college's reputational equivalency with "highly selective" and "national market" institutions in the region, but at identifying educational needs that the college was expected to serve. The strategic and master plans were not intended merely to manage the college's deferred maintenance liability, but to create a schoolhouse for the pedagogies that would provide access for the target market to their vocations. Structural reforms were intended to elicit departmental and divisional collaboration on which high institutional performance depended, not to create an effective command structure that would save the stumbling college.

Out of this planning work came a refined guideline for financial aid discounting, to secure an envisioned enrollment at a financially sustainable level. This profile meant consideration of new sources of net revenue from missional activities and mission-committed donors to make the college accessible to those targeted and to acquire instructional resources that were able to meet the educational challenges of the college's enrollment profile.

Although the inspiration for the institutional missions served by these two presidents came from very different sources, each mission entailed the effort to transform an array of constituencies into an academic regime composed of institutional partisans.

Eliciting Alumni Guidance about Envisioning

An experienced president who had come to the program on the verge of retirement reported that, after a debate, he had revised a major tenet in his understanding of his college's identity. He also had learned by conversation with peers and a facilitator in the Presidential Vocation and Institutional Mission Program to embrace and celebrate this revision and the improved presidency to which it led.

The college was in "real need of a turnaround" and had recruited him for the purpose. At the time of his selection, the trustees "were actually wondering whether to consider closing the place." Relations on campus, on the board, and between the administration and the trustees were "bad."

The new president decided to inaugurate his presidency by reforming the college's trademark core curriculum that had "played a major role in the intellectual formation" of every student who ever passed through the institution. He testified that it "had been of tremendous value in introducing [the students] to the world of work and the professions." It conveyed the founding denominational values of the college to students through both general education courses and courses in their majors. "But," he said, "it was so frozen that it could not accommodate the new needs of students who were just at or beyond the edge of the sponsoring tradition of the college. It was blocking these students and others who otherwise would have been enriched by it."

Even though he knew that "any change to the core curriculum was a declaration of war against the alumni and several of the faculty," he launched the reform to make the college more accessible and to raise enrollment. That precipitated a two-year battle. "A powerful chapter of the alumni that was associated with an internationally notable think tank led the opposition." Finally, he asked the alumni director to arrange a face-to-face meeting with the members of this chapter.

When they met, he offered a short statement about why he felt compelled to attempt reform and then invited questions and observations. He got plenty of each. Despite a tight knot in his stomach, he responded civilly and calmly. "By the end of the two-hour meeting," he said, "I had more respect for these people than I had when I walked in. The mood had turned very positive—because I heard what they said and they felt they had been listened to."

He went on to say that "my attitude towards the core curriculum changed that day. I didn't see it any longer as that doggone thing that hasn't changed in decades and that was preventing the college from getting the students that would help us balance the budget. I saw it, instead, as having shaped bright people who expressed their opposition in beautiful rhetoric and well-formed arguments, just the kind of people I was trying to supply as their successors."

The president reported that this denouement recommenced the envisioning process with different reforms. "I became more amenable to the arguments of the faculty senate. I stepped back from adversarial confrontations and got help from some of my critics in drawing the circle bigger. As a consequence, the president became a better spokesman" for the college and accomplished the turnaround with reforms that were more acceptable to the leading citizens of the college. The college wound up more energized, less altered, and a more cohesive community.

Restoring Founding Orthodoxy: Can It Be Done?

Another president came to the program deeply frustrated by faculty resistance to his effort to restore the college to its founding mission. He had been hired to bridge the gulf between the college's contemporary character and the original orthodoxy of its denominational tradition. This gulf had widened as successive presidents had accommodated regional demand for adult and continuing education programs, most of them in the professions. These accommodations had given the college strong growth and contributed to its financial health.

But the changes transformed what had once been a strictly under-graduate curriculum and culture into an elaborate mixture of programs and degree options. Long-standing faculty hiring practices to staff the emergent curriculum had yielded a workable alliance among men and women of varying faith commitments and educational philosophies. As the board and its new president saw it, however, the denominational identity of the school had therefore been compromised. The identity was only skin-deep, and that wasn't deep enough for either one of them.

This president had no intention of initiating an envisioning process from which he and his colleagues might together extract a compelling institutional self-definition. That self-definition had been provided at the institution's outset by its founders. It was no more the new president's vision than it was that of the college. In fact, it was an anachronism. Because there were inadequate remnants of it in the modern college, the president could find no purchase for his effort to reshape the college, and he was left with an impossible assignment.

By the time of the seminar interview, the president and his wife had begun to find the seeds of a new and effective vision for the institution in the stories of transformation occurring among its first-generation students, single mothers, and recent immigrants. As the children of immigrants themselves and the beneficiaries of a profound parental regard for academic enlightenment, they were finding in these stories evidence of the remarkable educational acumen of the college. And they were beginning to see these achievements belonged to the "new college," the one that had strayed from its founding. If this respect continues to grow in them, the "impossible assignment" may yet be fulfilled—by rec-onciling the principles of the college's founding with the transformative work accomplished among first-generation students by the institution's new, more modern programs. In short, the existing college is beginning to win the respect of the president. Some of that, at least, is a necessary condition of envisioning—as a collaborative process between president and institution—and is the first mark of the alignment on which depends productive and extended vocational presidencies.

Vocationists in American academe derive "deep gladness" from guiding their colleges into service of the world's "deep need" of educated, self-knowing, and self-aware citizens. This work is accomplished in every case reported here both close enough to the experience of the "hair shirt" to feel the scratchiness and far enough back from it to bear and sustain the commitment.

To put it differently and in light of the recurring testimony of the presidents and provosts quoted here, it is evident that some part of the deep gladness of vocational life lies in the burden of it. And that observation opens a route into one of the most complicated dimensions of the subject of vocation: suffering and its function in sustaining the burden, catalyzing both individual and institutional self-awareness, and constituting some element of the deep gladness itself.

Two further notes of caution should be mentioned. First, vocational joy is something like divine peace—it "passes all human understanding," and second, the axiom that joy depends inevitably on suffering has been challenged only in our time and then by our modern identification of joy with fun and entertainment, and of suffering with physical pain and mental illness. For their part, such Reformers as Martin Luther and others, who gave us in the sixteenth century a widened version of vocation, saw suffering as a generative process. Fun went unremarked among them—though they were certainly not without humor.

According to Luther, the isolating, even alienating, weight of vocational struggle opens the vocationist to the gospel promise of new life—but only if the experience is contemplated in the preserve of the Word and theologically grounded. For Luther, neither the vocationist nor anyone else among us can fully experience or fully understand the new life promised by the gospel. It is the faith-driven contemplation of the Word while suffering the alienation of unreconstructed human life that precipitates and sustains the reformist activity of the vocationist.

Conclusion

For many of the presidents whose testimony is recorded here, the equivalent vocationalizing tension is between personal and institutional purpose (drawn, respectively, from learning and founding), on the one hand, and an irritating, mysterious compulsion to actually realize those purposes in one's own and institutional life. To animate this dialectic in both personal and institutional life, the president needs an acute self-awareness and an institutional corollary of it. The self-awareness must entail enough self-criticism to establish and sustain humility and enough sense of growth and becoming to reach for and bear the burden of leadership. To enable a productive and mutually beneficial alignment between president and college or university, the institutional corollary of acute self-awareness must include some civilizing pride—in a founding that was to supply citizens for a free society; in a record of accessibility and transformed lives; in a nascent communal longing to be engaged in an institutional rather than individual enterprise.

Pulling these into discourse with each other and extracting from the interchange an institutional self-definition to orient hope and coordinate the too-often dissipating and unfocused energies of the college— this is the task of the vocational president. Such presidents are inevitably and consistently reformist, and they are working with their colleagues toward a community that is liberating and invigorating for everyone in it—students, faculty, and staff.

The effectiveness and joy of this work depends upon the level and degree of alignment between the president's calling, on the one hand, and the institution's mission, on the other. But just how is it that this alignment—when it exists—enables the deep gladness of vocational life for both the president and the college or university?

CHAPTER 5

Conclusion—The Alignment of Vocation and Mission in American Academe

The Presidential Vocation and Institutional Mission Program was intended to ease the burden and enhance the joy of the American college and university presidency. Judging by the reports of the thirty-five who, along with their spouses, were interviewed for this book, the program met or exceeded these expectations. Literally all those interviewed learned something new about themselves during the program that sent them back to their work with new zest for it. Those who arrived thinking about resigning returned to accomplish unfinished business.

The real surprise of the interviews was the source of the zest and extended tenures. Those presidents and deans who found new interest and fulfillment in their work found it in the underlying purpose of their work. The seminars did not provide presidents with more efficient, less tiring administrative techniques or leadership strategies. Nor was the burden eased by learning that others were bearing similar loads every day.

In fact, most presidents returned from their deliberations about personal vocation and institutional mission with a new conviction that their leadership of colleges in search of their own best selves could increase the institutions' contribution to the common weal. This conviction was grounded in the supposition that the work of the vocational presidency was a high order of community development and that the president was the key facilitator of this great undertaking. Without their role in sustaining the enterprise and holding the course, no such envisioning or alignment could take place.

The institutional leaders variously went looking for their own deep gladness and institutional vigor in overcoming departmental and divisional opposition to curricular reform, in establishing institutional interests ahead of constituent ones, and in bringing the college community together around a new or refined mission statement.

This distinctive attribute of vocation—that it energizes rather than exhausts, engages rather than isolates, enlarges rather than diminishes—would likely neither have been discovered nor explored in the academy were it not for the Lilly Endowment's initiative in 1999, the "Programs for the Theological Exploration of Vocation (PTEV)." The Presidential Vocation and Institutional Mission Program less than a decade later benefited from this earlier program, and its success supports the conclusion of several observers, including that of Craig Dykstra, the chief architect of PTEV, that vocation is an idea whose time has come: "What we thought at the beginning [of the initiative] might be nothing more than a modest experimental program ended up being a much larger and more significant part of the Endowment's overall efforts in religion than we ever could have imagined."[1]

Susan VanZanten from Seattle Pacific University has written that the "colossal success" of PTEV "stems, in part, from the way in which

---

1. Craig Dykstra, "Creating the Future: The Significance of the Theological Exploration of Vocation" (address to the Education for Vocation conference of the Evangelical Lutheran Church in America, Augsburg College, Minneapolis, Minn., November 1, 2010).

its ideas struck a timely chord in American society."[2] Both Dykstra and VanZanten seem to agree that since 1999 the high profile of vocation in American academe is due to a ripened cultural need of the concept and to extensions of the vocational idea that have been forged in the laboratory of the academy.

The Alignment of Personal Vocation and Institutional Mission

All the illuminating embellishments of this idea that came out of the more recent program depended upon alignment, a distinguishing aspect of vocational life wherever and whenever it may appear. This concept is what turns vocation into service to one's neighbor and, thus, to the immediate community in general. Without this attribute, there would be no telling whether a particular life or occupation was serving private or public purpose, whether an undertaking was prompted by ambition or a wish to be useful, or whether it was propelled by considerations of career or calling.

In every case encountered in the Presidential Vocation and Institutional Mission Program in which vigor and joy in leadership emanated directly from the work, the president or dean seemed aligned with four elements: 1) his or her own vocation; 2) his or her capabilities, both for personal and institutional discernment, and for the practical business of managing one's own and one's institution's life in a competitive environment; 3) institutional mission, and 4) the culture of the college or university.

Alignment is neither fusion nor merger, on the one hand, nor a loose alliance of independent forces, on the other. Aligned entities retain their separateness and achieve their shared orientation by a dialectical

---

2. Susan VanZanten, "The Stories of Our Lives: The Theological Exploration of Vocation in Colleges and Universities" (a paper posted at *Resources for American Christianity* http://www.resourcingChristianity.org).

interdependence through which they impinge upon each other to mutually beneficial effect.

The utility of vocation broadened dramatically for presidents and prospective presidents when they discovered that the terms and conditions of vocation could be applied directly to colleges and universities. Many leaders came to the Presidential Vocation and Institutional Mission Program looking for ways to ease the burdens of their efforts in the American academy. By the time the program inquiry turned to the subject of institutional mission, the participants had become convinced that having a clearly discerned calling was a great advantage in managing one's personal life. This advantage came most sharply into view in the informal and marital conversations about friendship. Many of those conversations apparently concluded that genuine friendship with others is a necessary condition of discerning one's deepest and truest self.

With vocation having won attention as potentially more fulfilling than a successful career or professional distinction, and with friendship established as a crucial condition of self-awareness, the turn of each seminar to a college's or university's saga" as a proxy for its vocation was profoundly exciting to both sitting and prospective presidents. Burton Clark's stories of the twentieth century invigoration of Antioch, Reed, and Swarthmore suggested that academic institutions might function as vocational persons, and further suggested that their missions might be the equivalent of callings, and their planning work (which we came to call "envisioning") the equivalent of our personal search for discernment.

The seminar group was profoundly excited by observing these equivalencies rooted, as the interviews revealed, in the need of many sitting presidents and deans for a raison d'etre for their leadership. They sought something higher than success in traditional terms, something that could vindicate the sacrifices that academic leadership exacts of peace of mind, family responsibilities, and easy collegiality. Clark's examples of institutional sagas did not reveal how to lighten the work or how to lessen the importance of institutional welfare in executive leadership. Rather, they showed that both personal fulfillment and institutional welfare may very well lie in the wholehearted embrace of the saga-telling presidency.

Our early exploration of personal vocation and friendship as critical instruments in discerning vocation had opened the group to such appealing aspects of vocational life as acute self-awareness, the satisfaction of duty well and truly done, and the thrill of liberation from the debilitating effects of modern alienation and social isolation by service to neighbor and community.

Against this background and especially for presidents and deans who had come to the program for relief from the strain of their work and to review the congruence of their lives and occupations, the prospect of the presidency as an expression of personal vocation as well as principal facilitator of institutional mission held an immediate appeal. The program conversations sent many back to campus with refreshed interest in and commitment to their work. It also sent them back with hope that they could help make their colleges more integrated, less compartmentalized, more self-aware, freed from self-doubt and ready to engage vigorously and self-confidently in service to the world, thus mirroring some of the same vocational transformations that were happening in their individual lives.

The excitement generated from the group's consideration of Clark's sagas was catalyzed by the idea of alignment in reflections about vocation. Congruence of the president's vocation with the college's mission—neither fusion nor calculated independence—promised a quantum of vigor for presidents and creativity for colleges that was available to either only through a dialectical and mutually advantageous relationship.

Seminar participants called this relationship between president and college "envisioning" and saw it as a distinctive operation of vocational leadership. For the group, it was much more than strategic planning or good administration. It was the literal opposite of visionary leadership in the sense that one's discerned calling through friendship transferred to the college. This envisioning sought the college's mission through the strategic, rhetorical, and administrative arts of alignment and the mobilization of the college in service to the community and the world.

The Dialectics of Alignment

A vice president, and doctoral candidate who was appointed to a presidency after participating in the program, found focus for his dissertation in the seminar's deliberations. His research concerned the relationship between academe's particular organizational forms and especially effective leadership styles. But the concepts in his dissertation regarding an understanding of the relationship between leadership mode and organizational form remained essentially theoretical.

By contrast, his practical experience as president transformed this orientation into one of constant feedback. From this perspective, the terms of the relationship between the organizational form and leadership mode appeared to be in motion, each modified by the other in an ongoing dialectical relationship. This relationship vindicated his conviction, as a self-consciously vocational president, that synchronicity of discernment of personal vocation and institutional mission is accomplished by the interplay of these organizational and leadership forces. At the same time he understood that neither entity ever loses its independence. For their part, the president and his spouse trace the high energy and hope they are bringing to the work directly to the integration in their lives of their education, their collaborative discernment of separate but mutual callings, and their shared diagnosis of the institution's circumstance and their aptitudes for serving its needs.

For them, the integration of these three factors also includes revision and refinement of their individual vocational discernment and of the college's understanding of its mission. This action constantly occurs by virtue of the feedback loop, modulating the relationship and keeping all factors within the hearing and sympathy of the others. Because the president and the college acknowledge that the self-definition and self-realization functions of envisioning contribute greatly to the benefit of each, the president has found deep gladness in this work.

As another president put it in describing his two principal take-aways from the seminar: "I have become more self-reflective about who I am and why I do what I do. And I've discovered that some part of who I am was given me by the college. I have become a part of the college's saga, part of its mission. I, myself, am becoming invisible to the college even as I become personally clearer about my identity."

Thanks to their great modesty, most of the participants in the Presidential Vocation and Institutional Mission Program easily accepted this inverse relationship that prevails between the high profile of the president and the emergence of an envisioned college. But they found it harder to remember that envisioning is more important than the college's possession of a vision.

Our insertion of vocational considerations into Clark's account of the sagas at the three colleges resulted in the realization that envisioning is an inquiring and deliberative art. As such, it seeks to extract a vision from the college community rather than relying upon the imposition of charismatic leaders with a flair for the dramatic. Even so, a couple of program alumni found themselves at the helms of colleges without much rudder. To stop their institutions from running aground, each propounded and began imposing a vision upon the adrift institution rather than collaborating with it in the patient business of envisioning. In each case, the institution's resistance to the attempt was so over-whelming that both resigned within a year of appointment.

A dean who had participated in the program realized in the final stages of a presidential search that he was contending for the position out of simple ambition. He withdrew from the search. Later, he secured a presidency that seemed to need his every talent. In fact, the college proposed to throw its very destiny upon him. He was thrilled by the prospect and yet sensed in his attraction to the position a serious danger that he would seek sole responsibility for the outcome—the glory of success as well as the terrible weight of failure. He accepted the presidency and is relying upon his self-awareness to maintain the border between his own and the institution's vocation.

A distant second for bringing a presidency to a premature end is, ironically, the opposite of the first; instead of a visionary leader imposing his or her vision on the school, this president drifts whence the institution lists. No participants in the program spoke of this experience, but the group speculated that such a situation may actually last longer, on average, than one that nobly and impatiently tries to restore an iconoclastic institution to its founding purpose. The group also supposed that the institution may be lost in the meantime, its purpose sacrificed to mere survival.

Vocational presidents hold that nothing including the actual possession of a vision is so critically needed in contemporary American academe as envisioning. And no leadership task is as fascinating to the vocational president as this one. As the vignettes in Chapter Four suggest, the program may have made its most valuable contribution to the "vocationalization" of America's colleges and universities in mapping out the process of envisioning, much more than through the articulation of any particular vision.

One president came to the program just after his selection by a troubled and shrinking college. As soon as he arrived on campus, he initiated an envisioning process that he designed during his participation in the Presidential Vocation and Institutional Mission Program. But when college finances continued to take a turn for the worse, he was redirected by his board to pursue a strategic plan. Laying aside the envisioning work, he developed a turnaround plan consisting of new net revenues and general expense savings. The institution's decline continued and triggered reductions in force that eliminated any remaining chance for new net revenues. The size of the annual budget deficits shrank and the college continued to operate in the red.

About two years after turning away from envisioning, the president was permitted to shift a significant portion of his own and the college's attention away from the immediate execution of the turnaround plan to the larger considerations of institutional mission. He and his colleagues concluded that financial planning alone would not secure the institution's future. Only a general mobilization could, which would require campus-wide agreement on a vision that reconciles the college's founding, its prevailing culture, and its competitive advantages. For the time being, he has won his board's acceptance of the proposition that this work comes before and gives birth to the strategic plan that serves it. While the long-term health of the college remains in question, the president reports that his own hopes as well as those of the board and his colleagues are rising.

Another president whose board challenged his reliance on envisioning to recover his college's financial health observed that "if the budget runs the university, or if the endowment or the development campaign runs the university, then the mission doesn't." And if the mission doesn't run the university, then survival alone is good enough. "In my view," he said, "the greatest power of a board is not hiring and firing the president, but reviewing, adapting, and authorizing the college's mission."

Given the absence, in this case, of a vision that draws the college's constituents together beneath a common flag, the presidency is almost entirely absorbed in managing a restive board and a resistant faculty that sees itself as besieged. "If the board allows itself in the name of fiduciary responsibility," said the president, "to tamper with the curriculum, it threatens the college's accreditation; if the faculty is profligate with the institution's financial resources, it threatens institutional viability." These threats in this case demanded the president's full attention. What he would rather have attempted—what he came there to accomplish— was "to find and commit the college to a vision statement that is institutionally self-energizing and, therefore, fundamentally self-funding."

This president agrees that only the board can work the college out of the immobility caused by its various misalignments. The only way it can do so, he believes, is to hire and prepare the way for an envisioning and vocational president. It took the first step in this case but not the second, and the question now is whether and how it will complete the task.

The Optimism of the Vocational Presidency

Those who took up or returned to their presidencies after participating in the program were anxious to employ their freshened understanding of the staple subjects of the seminar: vocation, friendship, envisioning, and alignment. Although every one of them confessed one frustration or another—with boards (which were interventionist or corporate in their approach to governance), fractious faculties, tradition-bound alumni, and/or careerist colleagues—they remained hopeful that their tenures would add to the health and serviceability of their colleges or universities.

This optimism is perhaps the greatest gift of the program to American academe. In several cases, it began among couples as they contemplated their joint participation in the seminars. Always, it grew by way of the curricular, informal, and marital conversations that flowered during the inaugural summer seminars and continued in the fall and winter seminars.

The collection of men and women holding nothing more in common than roughly equal rank in American higher education became a little community of friends in the course of exploring the possibility that human fulfillment might be found in one's work rather than in one's leisure. The exploration of this possibility involved consideration of personal matters that are only rarely admitted into social conversation—ambition vs. calling, self-awareness vs. reputation, self-confidence vs. arrogance. Even theological or philosophical matters in modern culture are often reserved for experts: To what are we called and how do we know? Is friendship a condition of self-knowledge? What are the personal benefits of a life of service?

Candid and confessional conversation about such matters requires trusting and caring partners. The Presidential Vocation and Institutional Mission Program created such partners and the resulting relationships greatly contributed to the optimism that presidents brought to their work before the seminars adjourned and even after everyone returned home.

The Vocational Presidency and the Reconciliation of Competing Forces

The envisioning template that took rough form during the seminars and then was adapted to each president's particular circumstance is insistently consultative. To some degree this is a matter of prudence: colleges are among the most profoundly democratized institutions of our times. Certain properties attend the title and rank of the college president, including prestige and certain perquisites of office. But political authority, the kind that mobilizes the members of a community to act for the sake of the whole, must be carefully cultivated by the president. The only vision that can mobilize the modern college or university is one that the college and its leaders have created together.

Consultation is a critical condition of this creation. In addition to accommodating the increasing demands of equality and inclusiveness and resisting the imposition of visionary leadership, consultation brings together the voices of the college's founders, the representatives of its current culture, and the diagnosticians of its competitive circumstance.

Into this gathering of voices, which is always a little confusing and some-times noisy, the president uses vocational thinking to find the intersec-tion of greatest harmony among them. She or he then adds scholarship and rhetoric to bring into view the vision, thus to establish institutional destination as the focal point of the college's emergent identity.

Several presidents who put the envisioning template to work on their campuses found the guiding idea of a clarified mission among the writings of the founders. Others found it among thoughtful alumni. Still others found it in the reflections of current faculty and staff on the rewards of their work or in the reasons for their loyalty to the college. None found such a seminal idea among the trustees, but every vocational president acknowledged that without board sympathy for, and sometimes active defense of, the process, envisioning would have been impossible.

The only image that can mobilize a college to undertake coherent and hopeful action for its own welfare is of a projection of itself that doesn't yet exist but some day very well might. Whatever the seed of its identity, this once and future order is more *gemeinshaft* (community) than *gesellshaft* (society). This hoped-for but not yet extant social order offers an alluring picture of connection and collaboration in place of the immediate reality of separation and competition. It is a dream that becomes realizable as the core notions of vocation strengthen their grasp on the imagination of the academic reformer and, through his or her leadership, on the civic culture of the institution.

Often the discovery of such an image somewhere in the history or circumstance of the college confirms the vocational president's generic conviction that every college and university of any substantial age once aimed to be some such community but wandered away from this com-mitment under the impact of a secular and commodity-driven culture. Such a discovery usually precipitates a burst of presidential scholarship concerning the original institutional distinction—whether achieved by the founders of the institution or later reformers of it—and the way in which certain modern forces have corroded it.

Here we come upon perhaps the stiffest challenge facing vocationists. Without a perspicuous criticism of modernity, the vocationist can advance no particular personal or collegiate strategy for living full and free in the context of that modernity. But the constant confirmations of the most clear-eyed criticisms regularly pushes the diagnostician to the verge of cynicism. If criticism of the world were to result in cynicism, vocation would be disenfranchised, and pessimism would amplify the fear that marks the presence of alienation in democratic times. How do vocationists find and sustain the hope—hope both for the modern world and for the college that lives within it—that is the necessary condition of their reformist and sympathetic engagement in its democratic (and alienating) processes?

Vocation as a Therapy for the Separations of Modern Democracy

Several of the program vocationists reported during the interviews that learning had both surprised and transformed them as young adults. One remembered the experience as an explosion of light, explicating the causes and consequences of some disquieting but mysterious trend or circumstance. Another remembered that a slower dawning had eventually freed him of the rustic simplicity and poverty into which he had been born.

As I listened to these stories of transformative learning, I could see the continuing influence of the reported experience in the animated inquirer sitting before me. These were not "successful students" who had "done well in school" and had converted their impressive transcripts into careers in higher education. No! They struck me as curious, wondering people, who had obtained a satisfying traction against the world. And they were people excited by a perpetual sense of being on the verge of a new truth about the human condition, already searching for ways to apply the discovery to the college and their work within it.

These people are acutely aware that the advancement of learning is neither naturally attractive to the human mind nor always particularly enlivening. Many would have agreed with a statement attributed to Mark Twain that "neither soap nor education are as sudden as a massacre, but, in the long run, each is just as deadly!" All of them have been forced to test their learning in executive institutional roles, and so they recognize the difference between idealism and realism. But what is most important about the vocationists among them is that they are profoundly interested in how and how much of the ideal they can insinuate into the real without compromising the ideal or allowing one to dominate the other.

A dean from the program who had passed up or withdrawn from searches for institutions that didn't "need" him said, after being elected by one that did: "The appointment has raised my self-confidence [and] given me the excuse I've been looking for to really go for it—to really use my talents and skills." His wife echoed this by observing that neither she nor the president-elect was in the least nervous about moving to a strange city and taking up new work: "No! We're at peace. We feel comfortable—as though we're just really coming into our own. It's liberating!" Among other things, the new president had decided to forego a standing invitation to rejoin a familiar and prestigious place in order to find what he really wanted—"the opportunity to work with persons who are unsure of their gifts; to be of help."

The public-service orientation illustrated in this vignette is altogether as liberating for the vocationist as was the lifting of social and religious restraints on private preference by the class- and privilege-destroying forces of equality of condition. And the personal reward of this liberation—in this vignette, to the full employment of one's talents and skills in the public interest—is actually more fulfilling than having one's particular personal cake and eating it too.

The CIC-Lilly program on personal vocation and institutional mission for college presidents and prospective presidents and their wives turns out to have been an exceedingly rich source for considering the distinctive nature of vocation, its applicability in our time, and its promise for helping us find alignment among the otherwise disparate parts of our lives.

In what other venue would we have so conveniently located the distinctions between career, profession, and vocation? Where might we have as candidly explored and reconciled to the appropriate degree the ambition of career with the summoned life of service, or the instinct of leadership with the high art of following? How else might we have learned that the only purpose to which an institution may be legitimately restored is one that is extracted from itself? Where else might we have seen that restoring an institution to itself entails a process that does the same for its facilitator?

In what other venue might we have seen a sixteenth-century concept emerging as the primary antidote to individualism and alienation—and without the debilitating side effects to the democracy which has hosted them?

The stiffest challenge facing vocationists is making a place for vocational colleges in the present context. Without an analysis and evaluation of modernity, the vocationist can advance no particular personal or collegiate strategy for living full and free in the context of that modernity. Vocational presidents need to find and sustain hope—both for the world and for the college that lives within it—as the necessary condition of pursuing the reformist agenda which distinguishes their leadership.

It seems to me that the most valuable gift of the program is a strengthened respect for the human need of sociality and of community service as satisfaction of that need.

Afterword

The most significant conclusion of the extensive inquiry of the Presidential Vocation and Institutional Mission Program is that vocation is the leading contemporary antidote to individualism in modern academe. The best statement I have seen of the difficulty of drawing any such conclusion was made by the Trappist liaison for novitiates in Pierre de Calan's remarkable novel, *Cosmas, or the Love of God.*

> A vocation is not open to empirical investigation. . . . Even those who, like myself, can say that they have never had the slightest doubt about their vocation, still feel overwhelmed and at a loss to explain exactly what this means. For here contradictory truths, inaccessible to ordinary human logic, come together; there is a sense of being led by someone stronger than oneself, and yet of remaining free; the feeling that the voice that calls us will never fall silent, that it will pursue us in season and out of season, and yet that it is within our power at any given moment not to heed it; the understanding that God has need of our cooperation to lead us wherever he desires. Mary was free to say no to the angel.[1]

---

1. Pierre de Calan, *Cosmas, or the Love of God*, Peter Hebblethwaite, trans. (Chicago: Loyola Classics, 1977), 37-38.

Facilitators of the Presidential Vocation and Institutional Mission Program (2005-2009)

Mihaly Csikszentmihalyi .... C. S. and D. J. Davidson Professor of Psychology and Management, Claremont Graduate University

Joel Cunningham .... Vice Chancellor, Sewanee: The University of the South

Trudy Cunningham .... Senior Consultant, Sewanee: The University of the South

Mary Ann Dillon .... President, Mount Aloysius College

Duncan Ferguson .... Director, Center for Spiritual Life, Eckerd College

William V. Frame .... President Emeritus, Augsburg College and Director of the Program

Anne Frame .... President's spouse, Augsburg College

Richard T. Hughes .... Director, Sider Institute for Anabaptist, Pietist and Wesleyan Studies, Messiah College

Douglas Jacobsen .... Distinguished Professor of Church History and Theology, Messiah College

Rhonda Jacobsen .... Professor of Psychology and Director of Faculty Development, Messiah College

Steven Jennings .... President, University of Evansville

James T. Laney .... President Emeritus, Emory University

Melanie Morey .... Senior Director for Research and Consulting, Catholic Education Institute

William C. Placher (deceased) .... Distinguished Professor in the Humanities, Wabash College

Jake Schrum ....President, Southwestern University (TX)
Mary Pat Seurkamp ....President, Notre Dame of Maryland University

Rich Ekman and Hal Hartley participated fully in all twelve gatherings of the seminars, and Fred Ohles, who developed the program application to the Lilly Foundation for CIC, planned and participated in each gathering until 2007 when he was appointed president of Nebraska Wesleyan University.

The Curriculum, Pedagogy, and Administration of the Presidential Vocation and Institutional Mission Program

The several meetings as well as the consultations of each of the seminars were guided by a faculty recruited as "facilitators" of the curriculum, not as deliverers of it. The planning team agreed from the outset that we would build the pedagogy around the participants' own observations and experiences. In fact, at the first and final plenary sessions of both the inaugural and winter meetings of each seminar, we insisted upon hearing from each participant about the prevailing question of the session. We tried to do the same in the small group sessions but without the "going-around-the-room" regimen required by the constraints of ninety-minute plenary sessions involving forty or so participants, facilitators, and observers.

We also agreed that we would elicit these observations and experiences by way of an intermediary reflection by the members of the seminar on a provocative reading. This helped us steer clear of the naval-gazing exchange of private testimony that some of us feared and led all the more effectively from the sophisticated exchanges in the seminar meetings to the intimate and profoundly meaningful conversations that I was privileged to hear about during the interviews for this book.

To achieve all these objectives, we recruited presidents and scholars of distinction as facilitators who were profound and knowing partisans of vocation and liberal education and hope-filled critics of such trends in American higher education as value-relativism, deconstruction, the disenfranchisement of faith, and the substitution of training for education. To facilitate the conversations with prospective presidents and their spouses, we especially wanted presidents, who had found their way into alignment with the institutions they had led or were leading; who therefore had found joy in the work; who acknowledged mentors; and whose recommendations would have weight in the industry. The leading requirement for all facilitators was their genuine interest in vocation, not only for themselves but also as a concept and strategy for the relief of the human condition in our time. I think we found them, as is attested by the list of facilitators recorded in Appendix I.

As often as possible, we chose classic texts for readings. For example, we used Aristotle's distinctive treatment of friendship as background for the determinedly equitable (and decisively public) marital friendship of John and Abigail Adams, or the classical understanding of civility embodied in Plato's *Crito* to help explain Lincoln's need for a "political religion" to reconcile self-interest with patriotism in a free society.

We also sought fruitful dialogue between religious and secular works. Hence, we contrasted statements from Luther, Calvin, and Bonhoeffer with those of Howard Gardner, Burton Clark, and Jim Collins—partly to help us recover work from its modern reputation as duty and drudgery and restore it to its vocational status as vitalizing service, and partly to reveal the promise of vocation for meeting the needs of modern colleges and universities for practical and effective leadership.

We were also anxious to find absorbing drama and poetry to sharpen our understanding of vocation and illustrate its presence in both special and ordinary circumstances. Hence, we were grateful to come upon Pierre de Calan's *Cosmas* and Robert Frost's "How Hard It Is to Keep from Being King When It Is in You and in the Situation." Readings like these widened our ability to spot the shoots and buds of vocation and mission as they first emerged.

These readings also helped us both bridge and distinguish the inaugural and closing meetings of each program year. These meetings were separated by five or six months, during which time two extensive one-on-one telephone conferences were convened by facilitators with individuals or couples to discuss an agenda collaboratively established first at Airlie House and then at Glendorn. (A third and final telephone conference completed the formal requirements of the program in the spring, approximately nine months after the inquiry began.)

Each seminar program, whether for sitting or prospective presidents and spouses, was reconvened for about two days during the winter. The objectives of these follow-up meetings were to hold a reunion at which we could record advances in our discernment and thinking about vocation, whether as participants or facilitators; to report changes or new directions in employment; and to identify and celebrate the achievements of the inquiry. Time and again, the great weight of testimony at the final session of the closing meeting ran first to domestic and collegial relationships established or improved during the inquiry, and then to the greater clarity of personal and institutional purpose that had occurred since the group first convened.

Hence, we relied much more heavily in these sessions than we had at first on literature that spoke directly to the individual rather than the president, the scholar, or the citizen. This seemed to encourage easy reporting by each of us of advances in our thinking or circumstance that had occurred since we had last seen each other five or six months earlier. (The celebratory nature of these winter meetings characterizes the program reunions that are now scheduled and hosted by CIC at the annual Presidents Institute each January.)

Throughout each of the seminars, we composed the participants into small groups of varying membership. Through these smaller groups, we sought to relate matters introduced in plenary sessions to the personal or institutional circumstance of participants. We normally constructed four so-called "permanent" groups of four or five individuals or couples and assigned to each a facilitator who was (or "were," where the facilitator was a couple) responsible for the two telephone conferences in the fall and the final one the following spring. The meetings of these permanent groups and of the one-on-one telephone conversations they facilitated served to keep the discernment and alignment processes running beyond the retreat and in the midst of the workaday world. The telephone conversations were understood to be subject to the same rules of discretion under which the book interviews were later conducted. These conversations played a major role in furnishing the closing gathering of each seminar with a strong sense of continuity with the opening session. They often also supplied facilitators with newly found friends who brought life issues to them for counsel.

Once or twice during both the opening and closing seminars of each program year, we gathered the spouses and the presidents or prospective presidents into separate groups. We did this both to affirm the spouses as full participants in the program and to create an atmosphere in which they could talk candidly about the challenges they faced or might eventually face in maintaining both personal and domestic life in a presidential household.

Finally, we mixed the members of cohorts to allow them to work at least once in both the summer and winter seminars with a new mix of colleagues and with a facilitator other than the coordinator of their permanent group.

All this variation in venue constituted a pedagogy meant to deliver the stipulated curriculum seamlessly and consistently. Each meeting was responsible for covering a segment of the curriculum, conscious of its place in the continuum of the inquiry. The facilitators pledged themselves to be especially alert to the discernment process occurring among the members of their permanent groups. We debriefed at the end of each day and summarized our expectations for the one ahead as the inquiry resumed each morning.

To encourage the extension of the inquiry that was occurring in private conversation, we used the two afternoons of the inaugural meetings to set the agendas for the telephone conferences to be held in the fall, and used one of the available evenings for strictly social and entertainment purposes. We adjourned no later than 9:00 p.m. each evening, and reconvened after breakfast at 8:30 a.m. As the interviews later revealed, many of the most valuable advances in discernment among the participants occurred in the private conversations this schedule permitted.

To market this program, CIC offered its membership a disciplined discernment exercise for both personal vocation and institutional mission in two compact meetings and four telephone conferences at nominal cost. During the course of the program's four-year span, demand for participants in the program escalated for prospective presidents, whose admission to the program required nomination by a sitting president. However, the interest of presidents themselves in the program abated somewhat after the first year. That led us, with Lilly's permission, to delay the third seminar for presidents by a year.

Several patterns emerged among the thirty-five individuals and couples interviewed for this volume. For example, twenty-five of the thirty-five interviewees were or had been chief academic officers. This was true of thirteen of the seventeen presidents interviewed and of twelve of the eighteen prospectives interviewed. The other six interviewed prospectives came to the seminar from student life (3), outside academe (2), and development (1). The four interviewed presidents who had come to the presidency from positions other than CAO or provost came from the professions (2), church administration (1), and development (1).

By the summer of 2009, twenty-two percent of the prospectives who participated in the program had been elected to presidencies during or shortly after their enrollment. All thirteen were interviewed for this book. Two left their presidencies within a year of obtaining them. Of the five other prospectives interviewed, three decided either not to pursue a presidency or to limit the range of institutions in which they might be interested. The two prospectives who remain committed to the presidency but so far unsuccessful in gaining one decided to defer seeking an external presidency in the hope that they would be drafted as successors to their own presidents in their home institutions. Three of the newly-elected prospectives took up the presidency in colleges with active faith traditions other than their own.

Representative Syllabus for the Presidential Vocation and Institutional Mission Program

Summer Meetings (2005-2008)

Session I. The Vocation of a College President

What is vocation, what isn't, and what sustains it?

> Twenty short readings selected from William C. Placher, ed., *Callings: Twenty Centuries of Christian Wisdom on Vocation* (Grand Rapids, MI: Eerdmans, 2005) and Mark R. Schwehn and Dorothy C. Bass, eds. *Leading Lives that Matter: What We Should Do and Who We Should Be* (Grand Rapids, MI: Eerdmans, 2006).

> Frederick Buechner, *Wishful Thinking: A Seeker's ABC* (New York: HarperCollins Publisher, 1993), 95.

> Lee Hardy, "Balancing Commitments: Work and Vocation," in *The Fabric of This World: Inquiries into Calling, Career Choice, and the Design of Human Work* (Grand Rapids, MI: Eerdmans, 1990), 111-118.

Session II. Vision, Mission, and Saga in Institutional Life

Can a college have a vocation? How can it be discerned?

> Burton B. Clark, "The Making of an Organizational Saga," in *The Distinctive College*, rev. ed. (New Brunswick, NJ: Transaction Publishers, 1992), 233-262.

What are the sources of your college's saga?

Jim Collins, "Level 5 Leadership," in *Good to Great* (New York: HarperCollins, 2001), 17-62.

How closely can and should your vocation be aligned with your college's mission, saga, or vocation?

Pierre de Calan, "Translator's Introduction" and "Chapter Five" in *Cosmas, or the Love of God*, Peter Hebblethwaite, trans. (Chicago: Loyola University Press, 2006), v – xiii and 55-67.

Session III. Facing the Challenges that Come with Vocation

What are the biggest challenges facing a vocational president?

Abraham Lincoln, "Address before the Young Men's Lyceum of Springfield, Illinois, January 27, 1838." Available online at: www.thelastfullmeasure.com/lyceum_address.htm.

How do you manage your biggest challenges? How did Lincoln manage his?

Abraham Lincoln, "Second Inaugural Address, 10 April 1865," *Intersection*, October 2004, p. 2.

Session IV. Finding Resources to Strengthen Vocation

What roles can (or must) faith and friendship play in discerning vocation?

Aristotle, "On Friendship," in *The Ethics of Aristotle: The Nicomachean Ethics*, J.A.K. Thomson, trans. (Baltimore: Penguin, 1953), 227-285.

What challenges faith and friendship in a presidency?

Richard T. Hughes, "The Vocation of a Christian College, or, What Makes Church-Related Education Christian?" in *The Vocation of a Christian Scholar* (Grand Rapids, MI: Eerdmans, 2005), 107-130.

What sustains faith and friendship in a presidency?

Abigail Adams, letters to John Adams on March 31, April 11, and July 14, 1776; John Adams, letters to Abigail Adams on April 14 and 28 and July 10, 1776. From archives of Massachusetts Historical Society. Available online at: www.masshist.org/adams.

Concluding Sessions

How do mission, vision, and saga intersect?

> Jill Ker Conway, "Choice," in *A Woman's Education* (New York: Random House, 2002), 11-24.

How shall we use vocation to "civil-ize" both the campus community and society at large?

> Plato, "Crito" and "The Apology," in *The Last Days of Socrates*, Hugh Tredennick and Harold Tarrant, trans. (New York: Penguin Classics, 2003), 31-70 and 71-96.

Winter Meetings (2006-2009)

Each of the seminars met for six sessions during the course of two days roughly six months after the initial gathering to advance and register the effect of the inquiry on the vocational discernment of participants. Presidents and their spouses met with facilitators at the CIC Presidents Institute in January 2006, 2007, and 2009. Prospective presidents gathered near the campus of Emory University in Atlanta each February 2006–2008. Facilitators had convened at least three conferences, usually via telephone, with each president, prospective president, or couple between the two gatherings and were to have convened another after the winter meeting.

Session I: What application have you made of vocational thinking since our summer meeting? With what result—either troubling or rewarding?

Testimony from all participants

Session II: How do "the muses" help with discernment? What do the following poems tell us about vocation, mission, or the alignment of the two?

> Poems by Vaclav Havel, "It Is I Who Must Begin"; Amy Lowell, "Astigmatism"; Rainer Maria Rilke, "Turning Point"; and Mary Sarton, "Now I Become Myself." Poems are readily available online.

Session III: What light does Frost shed upon vocation, mission, and the alignment of the two?

Robert Frost, "How Hard It Is to Keep from Being King When It's in You and in the Situation." Readily available online.

Session IV: How can applying for (or conducting) a presidency advance vocational discernment?

Diana Chapman Walsh, "Trustworthy Leadership," keynote address, Institute on College Student Values, Florida State University, February 4, 2005. Available at http://character-clearinghouse.fsu.edu/files/pdf/2005InstituteProceedings/Institute_2005_Walsh.pdf

Selections from Jill Kerr Conway, *True North* (New York: Vintage, 1995).

Session V: How do vocational presidents and their spouses remain committed to vocational life for themselves and for their colleges and universities?

Marty Linsky and Ronald A. Heifetz, *Leadership on the Line: Staying Alive through the Dangers of Leading* (Cambridge, MA: Harvard Business School Press, 2002).

Session VI: What do you hope will become of your college after you leave it? What are you doing about it?

Text excerpts from "Good to Great and the Social Sectors," November 2005, available at http://www.jimcollins.com/books/g2g-ss.html.

Concluding Session: What costs and advantages have you encountered so far in aligning vocation and mission?

Testimony from all participants

The Interview Questions

1. Look back, if you will, to the beginning of our Presidential Vocation and Institutional Mission inquiry. Some very rich conversation seemed to begin almost immediately. What was the moment when the inquiry really seized your interest—and why?

2. Can you think of two or three other moments during the inquiry when an idea or insight struck you as particularly useful—in your life? In your work? So far, how has the seminar helped you most profoundly?

3. Did the fruits of your engagement in the inquiry put you at odds in any way with the work culture in which you were then or are now engaged? Did those fruits help you to feel more or less at home in the collegiate (or other) community[ies] in which you live and/or work?

4. What experience have you had in helping your institution know and pursue its mission? If and when you try it again, what will you do differently?

5. What have you done to align your personal vocation and the mission of your institution? What have you found cannot be compromised in either vocation or mission for the sake of alignment?

6. What issues remain for the aligned vocationist in American academe? How are you managing these?

7. Will you encourage a respected colleague to enroll in the Presidential Vocation and Institutional Mission Program? With what caveats?

*These questions were sent to interviewees approximately one week before each interview.

CPSIA information can be obtained at www.ICGtesting.com
Printed in the USA
LVOW040702081112

306407LV00006B/1/P